12 GIFTS

FOR *Christ*

12 GIFTS
FOR *Christ*

TRADITIONS, ACTIVITIES, AND DEVOTIONALS
FOR A CHRIST-CENTERED CHRISTMAS

MERRILEE BOYACK

DESERET
BOOK

Salt Lake City, Utah

Library of Congress Cataloging-in-Publication Data

Boyack, Merrilee Browne, author.
  12 gifts for Christ / Merrilee Boyack.
     pages cm
  Includes bibliographical references.
  Summary: Discusses the Christmas season and the gifts we can give to Jesus Christ, including gratitude, obedience, and charity. Also offers activities and devotional ideas to help us—and our families—draw closer to Christ during the Christmas season.
  ISBN 978-1-60907-597-2 (paperbound)
  1. Christmas. 2. Mormons—Conduct of life. 3. Jesus Christ—Mormon interpretations. I. Title. II. Title: Twelve gifts for Christ.
  BV45.B69 2013
  263'.915—dc23   2013015367

Printed in the United States of America
Edwards Brothers Malloy, Ann Arbor, MI

10 9 8 7 6 5 4 3 2 1

To my mother, Hilda Browne,
who loves Christmas and Christ
with all her heart and soul

Contents

Acknowledgments

Christmas is a time of giving thanks, so I would like to take a moment to thank some important people in my life:

My family, who have always loved Christmas and have shared with me wonderful traditions to share with others.

I'd also like to thank the entire team at Deseret Book, specifically Jana Erickson, Lisa Mangum, Heather Ward, and Rachael Ward, who have been a delight to work with.

Introduction

It was Christmas night, and I was sitting quietly in the living room all by myself. I was tired—OK, I was exhausted. Christmas was done. Giant check mark on that one.

I sat in the soft glow of the Christmas tree and enjoyed its beauty. We had gotten a good tree that year. My husband insisted on a live tree every year and some were better than others. I enjoyed all the ornaments and the "thousand points of light" we joked about every year as my husband wound ten strands of lights around the tree.

Christmas tree—check.

I looked around me at all the nativity sets. I collect nativity sets and there were probably a hundred in that room all over the place. I loved each one and the adventure it took to obtain each set.

Nativity sets and decorations—check.

Upstairs the kids were playing with Dad. We had gotten the boys (including Dad) some cool remote control cars, and they were enjoying them noisily. I was so glad the gifts had worked out this year.

Gifts—check.

On and on I went through my mental checklist for my "Christmas To-Do List." It was Christmas night. The checklist was done. Christmas had been a success this year.

Or had it?

Somehow I felt vaguely unsettled about it all.

Don't get me wrong—I absolutely love the entire drama of Christmas celebrations. I love the decorations and the turkey with stuffing and the gifts for the grandparents and visiting with friends and family and attending the concerts and the parties and . . . *everything*. I love everything about the holiday season. And most of the time I even like to *do* it all.

So what was missing? Why did this Christmas night feel so . . . flat?

I glanced to my left and my eye caught on the big nativity set on the mantel. I saw the baby Jesus.

That's what was missing.

As a family, we try diligently to talk about Christ and focus on Christ during Christmas. But it was almost as if He just fell somewhere on the to-do list between the Christmas cards and the cranberries.

It was my focus that was off. And I was distressed that now, on Christmas night, the entire family thought, "Christmas: focus on Jesus—CHECK!" Like it was done. Like we were done.

That made me feel ever so sad.

I wanted things to be different. I wanted to find a way to turn Christmas into an experience focused on Christ. Not only that, I wanted to find a way to focus my family more on Jesus throughout the entire year. But how?

I prayed quietly in the dim light that Christmas night that I would be guided to find a way to help my family turn to Christ more fully.

And I kept praying.

The answer came four months later. It was a lovely day, and I was out on my daily walk. I stopped at my friend's house, and we were chatting in her living room when I noticed something.

"Whoops!" I said to Susan. "You forgot to put away a stocking for Christmas. It's hanging on your mantel." I was forever finding little things I had forgotten to pack away at the end of the Christmas season and assumed she had done the same.

"Oh, no," she replied. "That stays there all year long." I thought that was a little odd, so she explained. "Many years ago I was at my friend's house and *she* had a stocking hanging on *her* mantel. She explained that the whole family would write down a gift they wanted to give to Jesus and would put it in the stocking. They kept the stocking up all year as a reminder. Ever since, we have done the same."

I looked again at the beautiful white lace stocking hanging there and thought, "This is it!"

I went home and explained the idea to my husband, who smiled and nodded appropriately, probably thinking it was another one of my bright ideas that would fall by the wayside. But it did not. From that moment forward, I kept my eyes peeled for a beautiful stocking. Finally, I found a lovely small gold stocking with white trim. Perfect.

Christmas came once again. And on Christmas night, we gathered our four sons together. I showed them the stocking and explained what we wanted to do as a family. Surprisingly, they were pretty willing. We each filled out our card and put it in the stocking.

The days began to march on. Often at family home evening, we would refer to the stocking and talk about how we were doing on our gift for Christ. Sometimes one of the children would see the stocking and comment on it.

They weren't the only ones. I conduct a part-time law practice from my home and so my clients sit on my living room couch for our meetings. All year long, clients would ask what the stocking meant. Most of my clients were not of my faith, so it was a wonderful opportunity for me to explain how our family was trying to focus on Christ and were giving gifts to Him all year long.

The next Christmas came. Christmas night our family gathered around the tree and opened the stocking. By then, it had become almost like a treasured friend in our home. All of us talked about what we had done all year long to give a gift to the Savior. It was one of the most profound Christmases we had ever shared.

We finished our discussion, and the boys went off to watch a movie with my husband. Once again, I sat alone in the living room on Christmas night, enjoying the glow of the tree.

Things felt much different that year. The stocking hung on the mantel, full of *new* cards promising new gifts for the coming year. Truly, our family was now more fully focusing on Christ that season and throughout the year.

That year, the glow wasn't from the tree. It was from within.

A Gift for Christ

Christmas is a wonderful time of year when we contemplate the giving and receiving of gifts. Some of us may even start in January, planning and accumulating all year long. Others may wait until Christmas Eve to begin shopping. Many children begin thinking about the holiday early in the year and work on their wish lists with great care. We shop for gifts. We make gifts. We wrap gifts. And throughout the entire process, we hope that we can make someone we care about happy. It is a long-standing tradition of giving and receiving love.

But at Christmastime, we also contemplate the greatest gift of all—the subject of the entire celebration—the life of our Savior, the Christ Child.

Christmas is also a time to ponder the gifts given to us by our Heavenly Family.

Heavenly Father gave us the gift of life, the gift of the Creation, and then the gift that made it possible for us to become like Him and return to Him: His Son, Jesus Christ. The Apostle John described it beautifully:

> For God so loved the world, that he gave his only begotten Son, that whosoever believeth in him should not perish, but have everlasting life.
>
> For God sent not his Son into the world to condemn the world; but that the world through him might be saved. (John 3:16–17)

Christ then gave us the gift of His life. He told His disciples,

> This is my commandment, That ye love one another, as I have loved you.
>
> Greater love hath no man than this, that a man lay down his life for his friends. (John 15:12–13)

The Savior of the world—our Redeemer, the Prince of Peace—gave us the greatest gift we could ever receive through His atonement and crucifixion. He satisfied the demands of justice and broke the chains of death. By so doing, we can live forever and become like our Heavenly Parents and our Elder Brother.

At Christmastime, I think about Jesus and the gifts that He brought to me, and I have a great desire to give something back to Him. But what can I give? What could I give to Him, the creator of the universe?

I have pondered this thought with great longing to find an answer. As I ponder, though, I am filled with His love. I want to serve Him and do His will. Beyond that, I want to somehow give something to Him that has meaning for Him. Just as I search carefully for the right gift for someone I love, I search for the right gift for Him as well.

This book contains ideas for twelve gifts we could give to Christ. But we are certainly not limited to only these ideas. It is my hope that this will simply be a place to start.

Each chapter contains a personal devotional so you may have some quiet time to ponder each gift for the Savior and apply it to your own life. Each chapter also contains ideas for sharing and applying the gift with your family and children so you can give this gift to Jesus in a meaningful way.

I hope this book will be a resource guide for you to use as best fits your family. You may do everything on a personal basis. Or you may choose to have twelve family home evenings where the entire family focuses on one gift each week or each month.

However you choose to use the information in this book, my hope is that the stories and the ideas provided will bless your life and help you make Christ the center of your Christmas season—and your life.

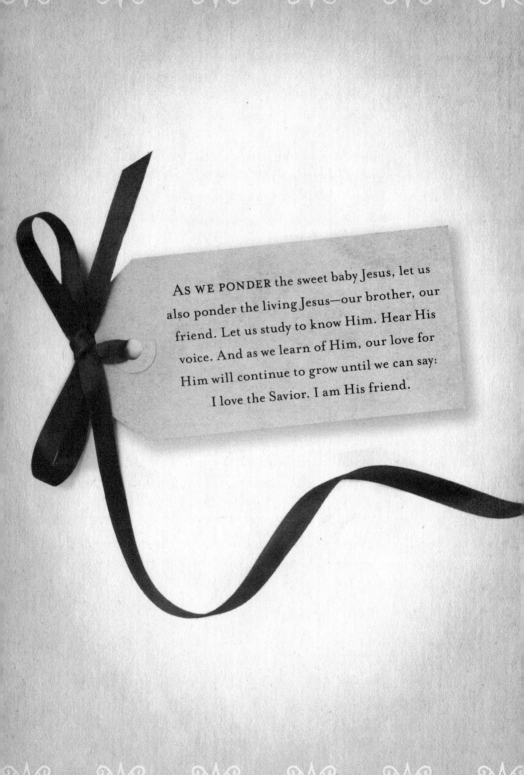

As we ponder the sweet baby Jesus, let us also ponder the living Jesus—our brother, our friend. Let us study to know Him. Hear His voice. And as we learn of Him, our love for Him will continue to grow until we can say: I love the Savior. I am His friend.

CHAPTER 1

The Gift of Personal Knowledge

Brennan, our second son, was about eleven years old and an energetic little rascal. It was Christmastime, and new neighbors had moved in next door. The wife, Susan, was confined to a wheelchair with multiple sclerosis. Brennan would come home from school each day, bouncing with pent-up energy, and I would say, "Brennan, Susan could use your help today setting up her Christmas decorations."

Off he would go in a flash. He would string lights and garlands, set up Santa and his reindeer, bake goodies—you name it. Day after day, he would help Susan.

A rather unlikely friendship developed between a disabled, middle-aged woman who was frustrated with her confinement and a free-spirited little boy who needed to be needed.

As we come to know the people around us, our hearts become knit with theirs. So it is with our Savior. As we increase in our knowledge and understanding of the Messiah, our hearts become knit with His and we grow in love for Him.

The Prophet Joseph Smith stated, "My first object is to find out the character of the only wise and true God. . . . I want you all to know God, to be familiar with him" ("King Follett Discourse," *Times and Seasons* 5 [15 August 1844]: 613).

To be familiar with Him. To know Him. To understand Him.

As little children, our love of Jesus feels innate. We love Him because

He loves us. But as we grow and mature, we realize that we want even more. We desire an understanding and a relationship that is deep and transcendent.

The scriptures speak to this goal and desire: "Learn of me, and listen to my words; walk in the meekness of my Spirit, and you shall have peace in me. I am Jesus Christ; I came by the will of the Father, and I do his will" (Doctrine and Covenants 19:23–24).

Christmas is a time when we can reflect on our relationship with the Savior. Our hearts turn to Him naturally. We begin our journey toward a deeper relationship with Him as we ponder Christ's willingness to come to Earth in such a humble way as an innocent little baby—so vulnerable and yet starting mortal life exactly as we did. There is a connection to this grand story of a little baby born in a manger that connects us to Him and to all our mortal brothers and sisters throughout the history of mankind.

But just as the Wise Men were seeking the Master, so too do we seek to find Him.

Elder Jeffrey R. Holland shares:

> One element is the question to every one of us, "What seek ye? What do you want?" . . . Whoever we are and whatever our problems, his response is always the same, forever: "Come unto me." Come see what I do and how I spend my time. Learn of me, follow me, and in the process I will give you answers to your prayers and rest to your souls. ("Come Unto Me," *Ensign*, April 1998, 16)

How do we come to know Him? We come unto Him. But what does that mean? Where do we start?

We turn first to those who have written of Him and read their words and their testimonies. We read the words of John the Beloved as he speaks of the Master, who was his friend. We ponder the words of Matthew, Mark, Luke, and more. We read the testimony of Enoch, who saw Him face to face, and we read the stirring testimony of Joseph Smith and Sidney Rigdon, who testified

> . . . the record which we bear is the fulness of the gospel of Jesus Christ, who is the Son, whom we saw and with whom we conversed in the heavenly vision. . . .
>
> And we beheld the glory of the Son, on the right hand of the Father, and received of his fulness;
>
> And saw the holy angels, and them who are sanctified before his throne, worshiping God, and the Lamb, who worship him forever and ever.
>
> And now, after the many testimonies which have been given of him, this is the testimony, last of all, which we give of him: That he lives!
>
> For we saw him, even on the right hand of God; and we heard the voice bearing record that he is the Only Begotten of the Father—
>
> That by him, and through him, and of him, the worlds are and were created, and the inhabitants thereof are begotten sons and daughters unto God. (Doctrine and Covenants 76:14, 20–24)

We read the scriptures for many things—to know what we should do, to learn about our past, to be guided and directed—but do we read them to come to know Him?

The Father has pointed us all to Him—His Beloved Son—and commanded us to hear Him. It is through Christ that we are taught and lifted up and saved. Christ is our Exemplar.

He draws near to us. And we can draw close to Him. We can ponder the scriptures deeply and pray for understanding that we may learn of Him. Who is Jesus? How does He act? How does He react? What does He enjoy doing? Finding the answers to such questions may help us as we come to know Jesus Christ, our elder brother.

I love that He calls His followers His friends:

> And again I say unto you, my friends, for from henceforth
> I shall call you friends, it is expedient that I give unto you this
> commandment, that ye become even as my friends in days
> when I was with them, traveling to preach the gospel in my
> power. (Doctrine and Covenants 84:77)

Do I know Him as a friend?

Several years ago, I was suffering greatly. I was going through the surgeries and treatments that accompany breast cancer when my husband lost his job. As I struggled, I turned to the scriptures for solace and understanding. I wanted to know my Savior more—He who had suffered for me and who offered me understanding and love.

As I read the scriptures, I discovered an insight I had not understood before. I read of how the Savior journeyed up the mountain to be with God before He undertook His mission. I read of Him walking by the seashore. And I read of Him going to His favorite garden often for respite.

Jesus, tasked with the most important mission in all of history, took time to restore His soul. He communed with God and went out into beautiful nature to seek peace.

In fact, the Garden of Gethsemane—which we often view with such sadness—was a place of peace and love for the Savior.

This realization sunk deep into my soul because I had done the same thing: when faced with stress and pain and just plain old fatigue, I often went to places of peace for comfort.

Somehow coming to know that He was like me in this way made my heart turn to His. As I thought about Him being tired and walking slowly to sit in the garden for a time and enjoying the beautiful plants and flowers and quiet, I felt such love for Him. He became even more real to me in that moment.

So as we ponder the sweet baby Jesus, let us also ponder the living Jesus—our brother, our friend. Let us study to know Him. Hear His voice.

And as we learn of Him, our love for Him will continue to grow until we can say: I love the Savior. I am His friend.

This gift of personal knowledge and love is something we can give Him. We can commit this day to come to know Him and to love Him.

 ## Personal Scripture Study

Read or watch and then ponder "The Living Christ: The Testimony of the Apostles," available at www.lds.org.

 ## Family Devotional

Each day for an entire month, read a verse about Jesus and see what you learn about Him. Select verses from the Gospels in the New Testament or from 3 Nephi. Ponder the following questions, or think of your own:

- What did He like to do?
- How did He react to things?
- What did He teach?
- Who were His friends, and how did He treat them?

Each evening, discuss as a family what you learned about the Savior and how you feel about what you've learned.

 ## Family Home Evening

Song: "Tell Me the Stories of Jesus," in *Children's Songbook* (Salt Lake City: The Church of Jesus Christ of Latter-day Saints, 1989), 57, or "Jesus Once Was a Little Child," *Children's Songbook,* 55.

Story: Read Luke 2 and discuss Jesus' childhood.

Game: "What Do You Know about Jesus?"

You could play this as a trivia game, a timed quiz, or as charades where you act out the answers.

What Do You Know about Jesus?

- When did you first know Jesus? (In our premortal life together!)
- How is Jesus related to you? (He's our eldest brother in the family of God.)
- Who was Jesus' father? (Heavenly Father)
- Who was Jesus' earthly mother? (Mary)
- Who was Mary's husband? (Joseph)
- Where was Jesus born? (Bethlehem)
- When Mary and Joseph took Jesus to the temple to be circumcised, what animal offerings did they bring? (Two turtledoves.)
- Where did He live as a little child? (Egypt)
- Did He have brothers and sisters? (Yes, but we don't know how many.)
- What trade did Joseph teach Him? (To be a carpenter.)
- Where was Jesus baptized? (River Jordan)
- Who baptized Him? (His cousin, John the Baptist.)
- Where did He live when He was growing up? (Nazareth)
- How many Apostles did He choose? (12)
- Who else were His friends? (Possible answers could include Lazarus, Mary, and Martha.)
- Jesus healed lots of people. What kinds of illnesses did they suffer from? (Possible answers could include blindness, deafness, leprosy, palsy, evil spirits.)
- Whom did He raise from the dead? (Possible answers could include Lazarus and the daughter of Jairus.)
- How many people did He feed with five loaves of bread and two fishes? (5,000)
- How did He die? (He was crucified on a cross.)
- What happened three days after He died? (He was resurrected.)
- Who saw Him when He was resurrected? (Possible answers could include His Apostles, a group of women, many people!)
- Where did He go after He visited the people in Jerusalem? (To visit the Nephites and Lamanites.)

- What did He do when He visited the people in the Americas? (Possible answers could include healed the sick, called His disciples, taught the people, and prayed for them.)
- To whom did He appear roughly 1800 years later? (Joseph Smith)
- What book of scripture contains His words and direction to the latter-day church? (The Doctrine and Covenants)
- Where does He live now? (With Father in Heaven.)

Activity: "Why Do I Love Jesus?"

Have each family member say one reason why they love Jesus. The next person repeats the answer and then adds their own. The next person repeats the first two answers and then adds their own. Continue until everyone has had a chance to participate.

Just for Christmas!

Display your favorite picture of Jesus in a prominent place in your Christmas decorations. Each day look at His picture and think of one thing about Him that touches your heart. Pray about it and then note your feelings in your journal.

Set up a crèche (you can use a simple, empty box) and wrap a baby doll to put inside to represent the baby Jesus. Cut out several small slips of paper. Have each family member write something they've learned or know about Jesus on a slip of paper and use it as "straw" for the crèche.

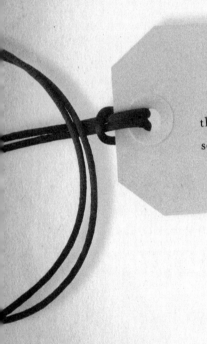

GRATITUDE is a place of hope. It's a place where we are thankful for the past and the present, and our thanks serves as a foundation for a future that is filled with hope and promise.

CHAPTER 2

The Gift of Gratitude

I sat at my desk with a pen in hand and a stack of blank note cards. I paused. How could I write these? How could I say what was in my heart? I had completed the first phases of my surgeries and treatments for breast cancer—and I was alive. I wanted to write thank-you notes to each of my doctors to thank them for helping to save my life and put my body back together after the ravages of cancer.

Instead, I just sat there and wept.

How could I say, "Thank you for saving me"? How could I say, "Thank you for the day you just patted my hand and told me everything would be OK"? How could I tell them, "Thank you for my life, for caring about me, for helping God cure me"?

Words were not nearly enough. They didn't come close.

I feel the same way at Christmastime. During the holiday season, I often like to sit in my living room in the quiet of the evening and enjoy the soft glow of the Christmas tree. I'm surrounded by nativity sets from around the world—all celebrating the birth of our Savior.

I think of Him, and my heart swells with gratitude. Thoughts and words just bubble up from my heart as I whisper prayers of feeling and thanks.

How do I tell Him what is in my heart? "Oh, thank you, Lord, for saving me!" How do I say, "Thank you for the time you came to me in the dark of the night, when I was so sad and alone, and filled me with love"?

How do I tell Him, "Thank you for my life, for caring about me, for rescuing me"?

Words are not nearly enough. They don't come close.

I am so grateful that He sees my heart, for my heart is full of thanks and praising for Him.

Gratitude is a wonderful place to be. I like to think of it as a place filled with "noticings"—every morning, we notice the sun that He made for us; we notice that we can breathe yet another day; we notice the little baby laughing in the store or the tiny flower peeking from underneath the leaf. And we are grateful to Him, the Creator.

Gratitude is a place of peace. When we are grateful, we are content with what we have and thankful to the Great Provider. Somehow, the grip of fear and doubt and pain and loss is lessened as we walk into that beautiful garden of gratitude, basking in the light of thanks for all that surrounds us. We take a seat and feel the breezes of peace wash over us, and we are thankful.

Gratitude is a place of hope. It's a place where we are thankful for the past and the present, and our thanks serves as a foundation for a future that is filled with hope and promise. We are filled with love for the Messiah: He who brings us hope by cleansing us and redeeming us so that we may rise up and meet our great destiny.

Mary, the mother of Jesus, had a great destiny—one she faced with dignity and grace. Think about all that she faced. She was young, was with child before she was married, and, because of that, probably faced a tremendous amount of gossip, judgment, and social rejection. Did her parents believe her? We do not know. Telling Joseph must have wrenched her heart, and the scriptures record that he was thinking about "put[ting] her away privily" (Matthew 1:19) until God intervened.

Her destiny was unlike that of any other woman in the history of mankind: she was to be the mother of the Son of God. She was to be the one who fed Him, clothed Him, taught Him, and cared for Him. It was her responsibility to be His mother. No doubt such a responsibility weighed heavy on her soul. And yet through it all, Mary was grateful:

> And Mary said, My soul doth magnify the Lord,
>
> And my spirit hath rejoiced in God my Saviour.
>
> For he hath regarded the low estate of his handmaiden: for, behold, from henceforth all generations shall call me blessed.
>
> For he that is mighty hath done to me great things; and holy is his name. (Luke 1:46–49)

In facing all the difficulty and adversity that she knew awaited her, Mary focused on God and on her gratitude toward Him.

President Thomas S. Monson shares his feelings on gratitude:

> *Gracias, danke, merci*—whatever language is spoken, "thank you" frequently expressed will cheer your spirit, broaden your friendships, and lift your lives to a higher pathway as you journey toward perfection. There is a simplicity—even a sincerity—when "thank you" is spoken. ("The Profound Power of Gratitude," *Ensign*, September 2005, 3; emphasis in original)

There is great power in both feeling gratitude and expressing it. During the Christmas season, we can give this gift of gratitude to our Savior.

President Monson also expressed his gratitude and love for the Savior:

> May I share with you my love for the Savior and for His great atoning sacrifice for us. . . . I believe that none of us can conceive the full import of what Christ did for us in Gethsemane, but I am grateful every day of my life for His atoning sacrifice in our behalf.
>
> At the last moment, He could have turned back. But He did not. He passed beneath all things that He might save all things. In doing so, He gave us life beyond this mortal existence. He reclaimed us from the Fall of Adam.
>
> To the depths of my very soul, I am grateful to Him. He

taught us how to live. He taught us how to die. He secured our salvation. ("At Parting," *Ensign,* May 2011, 114)

So to give this gift, we must first *feel* gratitude. Take some time to sit quietly and ponder the thankfulness you feel for your Redeemer. Let your heart be full.

And then we must *express* our gratitude. Say it out loud. Sing it. Write it. In whatever way or in all ways you want to express your gratitude to the Savior, let it free from your heart so that it may reach His heart.

Words are not enough. But they are a start as we give expression to that which we hold in our hearts. Praise His holy name with thanksgiving.

 Personal Scripture Study

Read these verses and ponder the importance of gratitude: Luke 1:46–55; Alma 36:3–28; 1 Samuel 1:11–2:21.

 Family Devotional

Read 3 Nephi, chapters 11 through 30. Read a few verses each day and talk about what you are thankful for and what you're learning. If your children are older, set a goal to read the entire book of 3 Nephi (one chapter a day) during the month of December.

 Family Home Evening

Song: "I Am Glad for Many Things," in *Children's Songbook* (Salt Lake City: The Church of Jesus Christ of Latter-day Saints, 1989), 151, or "I Feel My Savior's Love," *Children's Songbook,* 74, or "O Little Town of Bethlehem," in *Hymns of The Church of Jesus Christ of Latter-day Saints* (Salt Lake City: The Church of Jesus Christ of Latter-day Saints, 1985), no. 208.

Story: Have each family member share a story illustrating a gospel principle he or she is thankful for. Some family members may also choose to express gratitude for a time when they experienced a blessing in their life.

Some great scriptural stories on gratitude can be found here:

Mary, mother of Jesus: Luke 1:46–55

Alma, son of Alma: Alma 36:3–28

Hannah, mother of Samuel: 1 Samuel 1:11–2:21

Game: "I Spy" or "Scavenger Hunt"

Players describe something they see in the room that they're thankful for, such as: "I spy something very tall." The others players run around and point to the answer. (In this case, the answer could be "Dad!")

For older children, parents can prepare scavenger hunt-type clues and have the children search around the home for answers. For example, the clue might be "This is a great power God gives to all worthy men." The answer might be a picture of Joseph Smith receiving the priesthood. Another clue could be "This is a special place where families are sealed together," and the answer would be a picture of the temple. The difficulty of the clues will depend on the age of the children.

Activity: A "Thankful" Collage

Spread out a large sheet of paper or poster board on the table or floor. Provide a stack of assorted magazines and crayons or markers. Invite family members to cut out pictures from the magazines of things they are thankful for and tape them to the collage. Some family members may choose to draw pictures on the paper as well. Hang up the collage on the refrigerator or a blank wall.

JUST FOR CHRISTMAS!

Spend a quiet evening writing thank-you notes to anyone who has touched your life. Then write a letter to your Savior on lovely stationery and tell Him all the things that you are grateful for. Roll up the letter and tie it with a bow and put it on your Christmas tree or in another prominent place. Read the letter again on Christmas night. Keep it in your journal after Christmas as a reminder.

Set up a "gratitude" tree; small, inexpensive Christmas trees are often available at the dollar store. Set out a small box filled with slips of paper and ribbon. Invite family members to write expressions of thanks and gratitude to the Savior on the slips of paper and then tie them to the tree throughout the month. On Christmas Eve, pull the papers off the tree and read them together. Have family members keep the ones they've written in their personal journals.

AS WE REMEMBER our Savior, our lives have meaning and direction. We're not as distracted by the things of the world, and we can instead focus on others and the things that truly matter. It is through remembering Christ that we know what to do and how to do it. It is when we remember Christ that everything we do has virtue.

CHAPTER 3

The Gift of Remembrance

Our Father in Heaven has asked us to always remember His Son. Indeed, once we commit to baptism, we are invited every week to renew our covenant that we will always remember Him. We turn our hearts to Christ and tell our Heavenly Father that we will "witness unto thee, O God, the Eternal Father, that [we] are willing to take upon [us] the name of thy Son, and *always* remember him" (Doctrine and Covenants 20:77; emphasis added). We covenant with God. We affirm to Him week after week that we will *always* remember His Son and never, ever forget Him.

In the Book of Mormon, there are more than 240 instances of the word "remember" or forms of the word, including "remembered," "remembrance," or "forget not." This critical concept is taught over and over throughout the scriptures. A stirring reminder of the principle is given by Helaman when he was counseling his sons Nephi and Lehi,

> And now, my sons, remember, remember that it is upon the rock of our Redeemer, who is Christ, the Son of God, that ye must build your foundation; that when the devil shall send forth his mighty winds, yea, his shafts in the whirlwind, yea, when all his hail and his mighty storm shall beat upon you, it shall have no power over you to drag you down to the gulf of misery and endless wo, because of the rock upon which ye are built, which is a sure foundation, a foundation whereon if men build they cannot fall. (Helaman 5:12)

President Spencer W. Kimball said:

> When you look in the dictionary for the most important word, do you know what it is? It could be "remember." Because all of [us] have made covenants . . . our greatest need is to remember. That is why everyone goes to sacrament meeting every Sabbath day—to take the sacrament and listen to the priests pray that [we] "may always remember him and keep his commandments which he has given [us]." . . . "Remember" is the word. ("Circles of Exaltation," address to religious educators, Brigham Young University, June 28, 1968, 8)

Christmas is a time of remembering. We are reminded once again of the life of our Savior. We remember the miracle of His birth and why He came to Earth and what He did for us.

Author Emily Freeman writes of a time when she realized how critical it is to remember Christ at Christmas:

> December had come. The house was decorated, most of the presents bought, and Megan and I were driving in the car listening to Christmas carols. Strapped into her car seat and bundled up in her winter coat, Megan did her best to sing along. Then, just as one song ended and another began, Megan said one simple sentence that forever changed the way our family celebrates Christmas. "Mom," she began, "*I* believe in Santa Claus, and *you* believe in Jesus Christ."
>
> It was a moment of epiphany. I thought back over all of our holiday preparations and the experience we had created for our children. We had written letters to Santa, had talked about being good for Santa, and had counted down the days until Santa would come. We had spent the majority of the season teaching our children to believe in the reality of Santa Claus, and because of our efforts they trusted that he really would come. But suddenly I realized that we had not spent the

same amount of time teaching them to believe in the reality of the Savior. I thought over all of the traditions that filled our holiday season and realized that none of them strengthened my children's belief in Jesus Christ.

Since that moment, our home has been transformed into a home that believes. Not only in the magic of Santa, but also in the reality of our Savior, Jesus Christ, who is the true reason behind our celebration. (*A Christ-Centered Christmas* [Salt Lake City: Deseret Book, 2010], 1–2)

Do we remember Christ at Christmas? Do we remember Him *always*?

For me, remembering Christ means that in that moment when I'm tempted to continue sinning, I stop. I think of Him and how He has suffered for my sins and I decide in that moment not to add another sin to His suffering.

For me, remembering Christ means that when I am about to walk past that red bucket at Christmastime with the bell ringer smiling at me, I stop. I think of Him and how He has blessed me with abundance, and I donate a few coins to help others.

For me, remembering Christ means that when I start my day, I take a few minutes to pray and commit once again to following in His footsteps.

One day I read Moses 6:63: "And behold, all things have their likeness, and all things are created and made to bear record of me, both things which are temporal, and things which are spiritual; things which are in the heavens above, and things which are on the earth, and things which are in the earth, and things which are under the earth, both above and beneath: all things bear record of me." I thought about those words deeply. Jesus said *all* things—not just most things, or many things—*all* things testify of Him.

And so the next day I decided to look for Christ. In the morning, the sun rose, filling the earth with light and life, and I thought about how He is the Light and Life of the world. I saw Him when I looked at the sky and was reminded that there is a heaven and that it is His eternal abode. I saw Him when I looked at a little baby who signified new life just as He brings us to a newness of life. I heard Him in the music I listened to, the beautiful melodies reminding me of His beauty. I felt Him in the feelings I had for my children, knowing that I loved them as He loves us.

Truly all things testify of Him.

As we remember our Savior, our lives have meaning and direction. We're not as distracted by the things of the world, and we can instead focus on others and the things that truly matter. It is through remembering Christ that we know what to do and how to do it. It is when we remember Christ that everything we do has virtue.

At Christmastime, choose to remember Him in a real and meaningful way. Give Him the gift of holding Him close in your heart and mind. As we contemplate the birth of our Savior, may we always remember the life of our Savior. May we *always* remember Him.

 ## Personal Scripture Study

Read and study Doctrine and Covenants 20:75–79 and ponder the importance of remembering the Savior.

 ## Family Devotional

As a family, read President Henry B. Eyring's talk, "O Remember, Remember," *Ensign*, November 2007, 66–69. Talk about the ways your family can remember the Savior.

 ## Family Home Evening

Song: "I Lived in Heaven," in *Children's Songbook* (Salt Lake City: The Church of Jesus Christ of Latter-day Saints, 1989), 4, or "Stars Were Gleaming," *Children's Songbook*, 37.

Story: Invite family members to share their memories of things they remember from their childhood, about their grandparents, or even prior holidays. Talk about how wonderful it is to remember good things in our lives and how such memories can make us feel.

Game: Jesus "Memory Game"

Have children draw duplicate pictures of something they remember about Jesus; you'll end up with two matching pictures for each memory. If you choose to use full-size paper for the drawings, you can play a giant memory game on the floor of the room. If you use smaller index cards, play the game on a tabletop.

Mix up the pictures and place them facedown in a large grid. Take turns having each person flip over two papers, trying to remember where the matches are. When a match is made, the player gets to remove those two matching papers from the game and take another turn. The one with the most matches wins!

Activity: "O Remember" Bell

Give a small bell to each family member to carry in his or her pocket all day to remember Jesus. At dinnertime, invite each family member to share how he or she remembered Jesus that day. It could be a time when he or she was faced with a temptation but made the right choice. It might be when he or she saw something in nature and was grateful for His creation. It could be when he or she helped someone. Talk about how remembering Christ helps us live a more Christlike life. Then, as a family, ring your bells together.

JUST FOR CHRISTMAS!

Set up a nativity set by adding one piece each day. Write in your journal how each person remembered Jesus and His special role in Heavenly Father's plan of happiness.

Hold a family testimony meeting. Turn down all the lights and gather by the Christmas tree. Hand out candles to each family member (you can use battery-operated candles for young children). One person begins by lighting his or her candle and sharing his or her testimony of Jesus. He or she then lights another person's candle and that person shares his or her testimony.

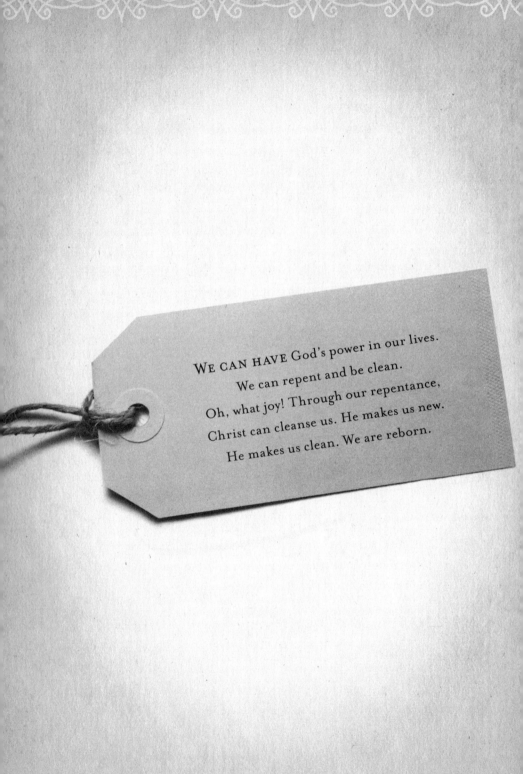

WE CAN HAVE God's power in our lives.
We can repent and be clean.
Oh, what joy! Through our repentance,
Christ can cleanse us. He makes us new.
He makes us clean. We are reborn.

CHAPTER 4

The Gift of Repentance

I was sitting in Relief Society listening to yet another class on repentance. Again? Seriously? Haven't we discussed this one enough?

Then the teacher began to talk about how *she* felt about repentance. Julie was a convert who had joined the Church in high school. She talked about how, as a child, she had been taught that repentance just meant telling the priest what you had done, and then getting some small assignment to say something and that was it.

Then she talked about being taught what true repentance meant, and she said something that forever changed how I felt about repentance. She said, "Never, ever forget the *joy* of repentance."

Joy? What did joy have to do with repentance?

Julie continued, "I learned that I could repent, truly repent, and be changed by the atonement of Jesus Christ. I learned that I could become a new person through Him. What joy that was to me."

I had never thought of it that way. I began to contemplate the beauty of that experience and was immediately filled with joy and thanks and love and hope! I could repent! I could change! I could be clean again! Oh, what joy!

But the natural man is tenacious. It's part of our mortal experience to have weaknesses. All of us make mistakes, and all of us sin. We are mortal beings in a sinful, mortal world.

Elder Jeffrey R. Holland said:

> I don't know what things may be troubling you personally,
> but, even knowing how terrific you are and how faithfully you
> are living, I would be surprised if someone somewhere weren't
> troubled by a transgression or the temptation of transgression.
> To you, wherever you may be, I say, Come unto him and lay
> down your burden. Let him lift the load. Let him give peace
> to your soul. Nothing in this world is more burdensome than
> sin. . . .
>
> You can change. You can be helped. You can be made
> whole—whatever the problem. All he asks is that you walk
> away from the darkness and come into the light, his light,
> with meekness and lowliness of heart. That is at the heart
> of the gospel. That is the very center of our message. That is
> the beauty of redemption. Christ has "borne our griefs, and
> carried our sorrows," Isaiah declared, "and with his stripes we
> are healed"—if we want to be. (Isa. 53:4–5; see also Mosiah
> 14:4–5.) ("Come Unto Me," *Ensign,* April 1998, 18)

Now it may seem a bit strange to think of our repentance as a gift. How
can our changing, our repenting, be a gift for Him?

Then I think of my children. I want my children to be happy and I
know that if they are striving to be the best they can be, then they will be
happy. So how can my children be the *best* they can be? Certainly, there
are things holding them back in their lives; there are things they are doing
that are preventing them from rising up to their full potential. They are no
different from anyone else on the planet.

I also know that sins—those actions and behaviors that violate God's
laws—are particularly damaging to our ability to progress and be our best.
So it makes sense that to stop sinning would be critical to our progression.

But stopping is not enough. Due to the demands of justice and the
effects of mortal sin, just stopping does not mean we are free. Stopping is
just one step in the process. To complete a full repentance, we must involve

God. Once we go through the repentance process and turn back to God's path, we are able to progress again along the path that leads to our best self and to happiness.

Jesus wants us to be happy. He wants us to become like Him and live as He did so that we can be our best selves. He offers us forgiveness and cleansing so that we can move forward in our process of becoming like Him.

He wants all of this because of His great love for us. He has suffered for us so He already knows the pain our sins cause us. He already knows how terrible we feel about ourselves when we persist in sinning. He already knows, and still He extends His loving arms to us. He says, "Oh, child. I know. I have felt what you're feeling. I can help. Please, just come unto me."

Repentance is a gift we can give to Him. He desires our repentance with all of His being.

There is immense beauty in repentance. We can turn to Him and ask Him to change us. We can seek a new life, a fresh start. Whatever wrongs we have done or are doing, we can stop! And as we stop and remember Christ, we can turn back to Him and tell Him, "I don't want to *be* this way anymore."

Then we can bask in His light and His love for us and in His vision of who we can become. We can begin again, freed from whatever it was that was holding us back. Cleansed from all things, we can begin to move forward once more, holding true to our path in life and to our destiny that awaits us.

> For verily I say unto you, I will that ye should overcome the world; wherefore I will have compassion upon you.
>
> There are those among you who have sinned; but verily I say, for this once, for mine own glory, and for the salvation of souls, I have forgiven you your sins.
>
> I will be merciful unto you, for I have given unto you the kingdom. . . .

. . . I, the Lord, forgive sins unto those who confess their sins before me and ask forgiveness, who have not sinned unto death. (Doctrine and Covenants 64:2–4, 7)

We all have sins. The Lord just asks that we repent of them—however many times that takes.

We can have God's power in our lives. We can repent and be clean. Oh, what joy! Through our repentance, Christ can cleanse us. He makes us new. He makes us clean. We are reborn. To feel clean again is such a thrill. That is the gift of repentance.

So let us take those first steps to turn to Him and ask Him to walk with us on the path of repentance. He will love such a gift.

 Personal Scripture Study

Read Doctrine and Covenants 64—especially verses 1–11—and ponder repentance.

 Family Devotional

Read the story of Alma the Younger and the sons of Mosiah in Mosiah 27:1–28:9. Discuss how they changed their lives when they repented and how the Lord used them to teach the Lamanites about repentance.

 Family Home Evening

Song: "Come unto Jesus," in *Hymns of The Church of Jesus Christ of Latter-day Saints* (Salt Lake City: The Church of Jesus Christ of Latter-day Saints, 1985), no. 117, or "He Sent His Son," in *Children's Songbook* (Salt Lake City: The Church of Jesus Christ of Latter-day Saints, 1989), 34.

Story: Benjamin Learns to Repent

And it came to pass that Benjamin, son of Joshua and

Leala, who was the sister of Nephi, dug along the bottom of the creek with his fingers. "Ah, a good one!" he exclaimed and pulled out a smooth, round stone. He examined it closely. "This one is special!" he said as he noticed a red line running through the middle of the rock.

He added the rock to the small pile by the side of the creek. He climbed out of the creek and scooped up the small pile of rocks. What a fine collection he had! He had about twelve rocks: some gray, some black, two white ones, and now his special rock with the red stripe. All were smooth and round from being in the water.

Benjamin excitedly put them into the leather pouch that was tied at his waist. He scrambled up the bank of the creek and sprinted across the meadow. Soon he reached his village.

"There you are, my little rascal!" called his mother. "Where have you been?"

"I was collecting rocks," explained Benjamin.

"Rocks, rocks, rocks. You must have rocks in your head!" She laughed and rubbed his black hair that never seemed to lay flat. "It's time for your chores," said his mother as she carried the basket of grain toward the village.

"Yes, Mother," said Benjamin. He ran off to get the water pots. It was his job to get fresh water for the family. He had forgotten to take them along in his excitement to gather new rocks.

Benjamin worked quickly filling the water pots and gathering sticks for the fire. He fed and watered the animals and helped his father cut wood for the family to use.

Soon it was time for the little children to take their naps. But Benjamin was too excited to sleep. He snuck out of his tent and walked quietly to the edge of the village.

Ah, trees! Benjamin's favorite thing to do was to throw

rocks. He threw rocks at big rocks. He threw rocks over the edge of the big hill at the other end of the village. He threw rocks into the creek. But he loved to throw rocks at trees most of all. He would pick a spot on the tree and try to hit that spot with his rock.

The men in the family had slings to throw their rocks, but Benjamin was still too young to have a sling. He was just as happy throwing rocks.

He had heard the story of David and the giant Goliath. He had learned how young David had killed the giant with his sling and his rocks and saved the Israelite nation. Benjamin wanted to be the best rock thrower ever so that when he got a sling, he would have the best aim of anyone.

Benjamin saw a skinny tree and threw a few rocks at the dark spot on the tree. Ping—ping! The rocks hit the target easily.

Benjamin walked on looking for harder targets. Up the path, he saw the temple on the hill. He walked toward the large building.

Uncle Nephi and the men of the family were building a large temple. He had been told that it was like the temple of Solomon back in Jerusalem, but he didn't quite understand that. It was the biggest building he had ever seen.

Oh, but look! There was something new! A tall column of wood was in front of the temple. It stood so high, Benjamin had to shield his eyes from the sun to see it all. It was as tall as two men!

But what was really special was what was on the wood. Carved up and down the front of the wooden pillar were many big circles, one after another. Zoram must have carved them, thought Benjamin. Zoram was a great woodcarver.

Benjamin stared up at the big carved circles on the tall

pillar of wood. And a thought came to his mind. "Oh, they're the perfect targets!" said Benjamin. And before he could think another thought, he backed up and began to throw his rocks at the circles.

Over and over and higher and higher, he threw his rocks. As he would go to pick them up, he noticed little dents in the wood pillar. But he ignored them and kept throwing his rocks.

After a long time, he grew tired and walked over to a tree beside the temple and curled up to take a nap.

"Hey, sleepyhead!" Someone was nudging Benjamin with his toe. "What are you doing here?"

Benjamin looked up to see his Uncle Nephi standing over him. "Oh, I couldn't sleep and came here," said Benjamin, and then he shut his lips tight.

His Uncle Nephi sat beside him. "Well, I can't think of a better place to take a nap. This is a sacred place. We will finish building the temple today and tomorrow we will dedicate it to the Lord."

"What?" asked Benjamin.

"That is when I will say an important prayer, and then this temple will be the House of the Lord. It will be His house and always a sacred place for our people. We will worship the Lord here," explained Uncle Nephi.

"You mean it's really God's house?" asked Benjamin. "Is He going to live there?"

Uncle Nephi chuckled. "Well, yes, in a certain way. This is where we can be with Him and worship Him. He lives in Heaven, but this will be one of His special houses on our land. It will be His temple."

Benjamin felt terrible. "Why the sad face?" asked Uncle Nephi.

"Oh, nothing," said Benjamin. "I better get back." He rose slowly and walked down the hill.

As he walked, Benjamin felt heavier and heavier. What have I done? he thought. He didn't feel like going back to his home and turned to the woods. He sat by the creek. I have been throwing rocks at God's house, he thought, and I left dents in that beautiful pillar in front of the temple. Benjamin felt so sad.

Soon, great tears welled up in Benjamin's eyes and he began to sob. "Oh, what have I done? That was so bad," he cried. After a time, he stopped crying and thought, What can I do now?

Then Benjamin remembered that his father had taught him about repentance. His father had said, "If you do something that you know is wrong, you need to repent. You need to say you are sorry and then try to fix whatever you did wrong. Then ask Heavenly Father to forgive you and He will."

Oh, thought Benjamin, I am so very sorry. So he knelt in the soft sand by the creek and prayed. "Heavenly Father, I am so, so sorry about throwing rocks at the temple. I should never have thrown them at Thy house. And I feel so bad about leaving dents. I will never throw rocks at things that can be hurt ever again. Please forgive me." Benjamin cried a little bit more. "Please forgive me, Heavenly Father. I will try to be a good boy from now on."

Then Benjamin stood when he was done praying. He felt a little bit better. He walked toward the temple. As he walked, he felt better and better. He reached the big wooden pillar. He looked up at the pillar and felt a little sad again.

Zoram stood by his side. "Wonderful, isn't it?" he asked, placing his big hand on Benjamin's shoulders.

"Oh, yes, it is beautiful," said Benjamin. "And I am so very sorry."

"But why?" asked Zoram. Benjamin walked over to the giant pillar and ran his hand softly over the small dents.

"I threw rocks at the pillar," whispered Benjamin softly. "And I feel really bad about it."

Zoram's hand rested on his shoulders again. "Would you like to fix it?" he asked.

"Oh, yes!" exclaimed Benjamin. "Can I?"

Zoram smiled and handed him a small tool. "Just take this and move it over all the dents and they will go away."

Benjamin began to work, smoothing all the dents in the large pillar. After much time and effort, he stood back to look at his work. "I can't even see them," he said.

Zoram came over and stood by his side. "Good work, Benjamin. I'm proud of you. I would like to teach you more about woodcarving if you would like to learn."

"Oh, yes, I would. Thanks!" replied Benjamin.

The next day the family all gathered around the temple. Nephi asked them all to be seated, and he began to pray. As he prayed and talked to the Lord and asked Him to accept the temple that they had all worked hard to build, Benjamin felt a sweet peace in his heart. He knew that the Lord had forgiven him. "Oh, thank you!" he whispered in prayer to his Heavenly Father.

And it came to pass that Benjamin had learned that repentance helped him feel better and that he could fix his mistakes. He had learned that Heavenly Father would forgive him if he would repent. Benjamin peeked up at the tall beautiful pillar in front of the temple. And he felt happy. (Merrilee Browne Boyack, *Book of Mormon Children* [Springville, Utah: Cedar Fort, 2012], 9. Used by permission of Cedar Fort, Inc.)

Game: "Marco Polo"

Blindfold a family member and have him or her call out "Marco." The other family members respond by saying "Polo." (For a fun variation, you can use any word or name combination such as "Merry" and "Christmas" or "Joseph" and "Smith" or "Mary" and "Joseph.") The blindfolded person tries to catch one of the other players. The tagged player then takes a turn with the blindfold.

Depending on the age of the children involved, you can also play this game in the backyard at night when it's dark. No blindfold needed! Another variation is to darken the entire house and play throughout the house.

As you play, reinforce the concept of turning to those who can help you when you're in the dark—especially Jesus!

Activity: Sin Is Erased!

On a small whiteboard, invite family members to write down a list of things for which a person might need to seek repentance. After you complete a list, discuss the principles of repentance and then ask a child to erase the list completely. Talk about how repentance can leave you clean and pure.

JUST FOR CHRISTMAS!

Purchase a special ornament ball that has either an image of the Savior on it or a picture of the temple. (You could also make one by slipping a small picture of Christ or the temple into a clear glass ornament ball.)

Gently pull off the top of the ornament. On a small slip of paper, write down one sin you would like to repent of and ways in which the Savior can help you accomplish your goal. Place the slip of paper into the ball and replace the top. Hang the ornament on your tree. Every time you see that specific ornament, pray for help to complete your repentance and be free of this sin.

Buy a white ornament for each member of the family. Using permanent marker, have each family member write his or her name on the ornament. As you hang the ornaments on the tree, talk about how the color white symbolizes purity and that purity comes through repentance. Testify that we can stay clean through the power of Christ's atonement.

WHEN WE CHOOSE to obey God,
we are choosing to bend our own personal
will to His. It is the ultimate gift to Him.
Just as the Savior bent His will to the Father's,
so we must choose to bend our will to His.

CHAPTER 5

The Gift of Obedience

When I think of obedience, I think of skiing. Sometimes, one of my skis will just slowly drift off the straight track. It doesn't take too long for that to become dangerous and painful! (One time I was skiing in deep powder and let one ski drift. Soon I found myself rolling head over heels down a mountain!) Other times, a ski can catch a sharp edge in the snow and jump off the track. Both examples are very serious, and a good skier tries to fix the problem immediately.

Obedience is like that. Sometimes we get a little casual, a little lazy, and we allow a small disobedience to creep into our lives and we start to drift. Sometimes we commit a clear sin that jolts our spiritual progress off track. Both are dangerous. Both need constant vigilance to prevent them from happening.

We might keep most of our behavior in good order, going forward and staying on track, but we know that there is one thing, or perhaps a few things, in our lives that is not in control. Sometimes we resist the efforts of the Spirit to correct us and stubbornly hang on to that particular sin or behavior. We know it's wrong, but we're just so resistant to change!

Obedience is a great blessing for us. The Lord looks on us and says, "You can be happier. You can be better. Here's how!" He repeatedly gives us commandments—simple, straightforward, and clear commandments—and then promises us that He will bless us and we will be happier, we will be better.

King Benjamin taught his people about this wonderful cycle of obedience and blessing.

> And behold, all that he requires of you is to keep his commandments; and he has promised you that if ye would keep his commandments ye should prosper in the land; and he never doth vary from that which he hath said; therefore, if ye do keep his commandments he doth bless you and prosper you.
>
> And now, in the first place, he hath created you, and granted unto you your lives, for which ye are indebted unto him.
>
> And secondly, he doth require that ye should do as he hath commanded you; for which if ye do, he doth immediately bless you; and therefore he hath paid you. And ye are still indebted unto him, and are, and will be, forever and ever; therefore, of what have ye to boast? (Mosiah 2:22–24)

The Christmas story is filled with wonderful examples of obedience as well. Mary, when told by an angel that she was to become the mother of the Son of God, responded, "Behold the handmaid of the Lord; be it unto me according to thy word" (Luke 1:38).

Joseph also reacted with obedience:

> But while he thought on these things, behold, the angel of the Lord appeared unto him in a dream, saying, Joseph, thou son of David, fear not to take unto thee Mary thy wife: for that which is conceived in her is of the Holy Ghost.
>
> And she shall bring forth a son, and thou shalt call his name JESUS: for he shall save his people from their sins. . . .
>
> Then Joseph being raised from sleep did as the angel of the Lord had bidden him, and took unto him his wife:
>
> And knew her not till she had brought forth her firstborn son: and he called his name JESUS. (Matthew 1:20–21, 24–25)

It's no wonder that Mary and Joseph were chosen to be Christ's earthly parents. They were faithfully obedient.

Others in the Christmas story were obedient as well. The shepherds were obedient to the vision they had received: "And they came with haste, and found Mary, and Joseph, and the babe lying in a manger" (Luke 2:16). I love that the shepherds went "with haste." There was no dillydallying going on!

The Wise Men also obeyed the direction they received after they had visited the young Jesus: "And being warned of God in a dream that they should not return to Herod, they departed into their own country another way" (Matthew 2:12).

Many stories of obedience flow through the scriptures to teach us and inspire us. They are not stories of perfect people. They are stories of imperfect men and women striving to be obedient as much as they could. Only the Savior lived a perfect life, and there is much we can learn about obedience from His life as well.

Ultimately, I believe that obedience boils down to trust and personal will. Do we trust God? Do we trust that He knows what is best for us? Do we trust Him no matter what we can or cannot see down the road? This is a serious question that is the foundation of all obedience.

If we trust God, then we have a choice. We can obey Him or not. Elder Neal A. Maxwell said:

> What keeps us from knowing and loving Him more? Our reluctance to give away all our sins—thinking, instead, a down payment will do. Likewise, our reluctance to let our wills be swallowed up in His will—thinking, instead, that merely acknowledging His will is sufficient! ("Encircled in the Arms of His Love," *Ensign,* November 2002, 18)

When we choose to obey God, we are choosing to bend our own personal will to His. It is the ultimate gift to Him. Just as the Savior bent His will to the Father's, so we must choose to bend our will to His.

Our own obedience is a deeply personal thing. The only ones who know truly how well we are doing—or even what we are doing with our own obedience—are the Father and the Son. They see our private moments where we are tested and triumphant. They see the times when we choose to be honest when no one else knows. They know when we overcome temptation and choose obedience.

Our obedience is a gift we can give Jesus. We can commit today—in this very moment, even—to be obedient with exactness. Choose to bend your will to the Savior's in complete obedience. That is a gift He will treasure.

 ## Personal Scripture Study

Read Luke 1 about Mary and Elisabeth and their obedience to the Lord.

 ## Family Devotional

Read about Nephi's obedience in 1 Nephi 3–5. Discuss not only how Nephi was blessed for his obedience, but how future generations were blessed because of his actions. As a family, memorize 1 Nephi 3:7.

 ## Family Home Evening

Song: "Keep the Commandments," in *Hymns of The Church of Jesus Christ of Latter-day Saints* (Salt Lake City: The Church of Jesus Christ of Latter-day Saints, 1985), no. 303, or "Angels We Have Heard on High," in *Hymns,* no. 203.

Story: Invite family members to share experiences of when they were obedient. Parents could talk about serving a mission or being sealed in the temple. Children could talk about a time when they did what they were told. As a family, discuss how each person felt when he or she was obedient and what blessings came as a result.

Game: "Shepherd Simon Says"

One person is the leader (for fun, you can dress up as a shepherd) and tells everyone to do the same action—but only when Shepherd Simon says.

The rest of the players continue to do the action until the leader gives them another instruction.

The leader should occasionally slip in an instruction without saying the words, "Shepherd Simon Says." The players who perform that action are out of the game. The winner is the last player remaining who has *only* done the actions that Simon said to do!

For a fun Christmas twist on this game, include actions that reflect Christmas traditions (for example, stir the cookie dough, reach for the top of the tree, jump through the snow, etc.).

Activity: Family Project

Do a family project together that involves following directions. For example, the family could clean a room together with Mom or Dad giving instructions to the children. An even larger project could be painting a room or assembling a piece of furniture. As a family, discuss how important it is to be obedient to directions. Talk about how the project might have turned out if someone was not obedient.

JUST FOR CHRISTMAS!

Set a goal to increase your personal spiritual obedience. For example, you might decide to read your scriptures for five minutes a day, or pray on your knees twice a day, or write in your journal daily. Practice that habit perfectly for a week (or longer if you'd like).

When you've finished your perfect week, treat yourself to a "Christmas Blessing." This could be a trinket from the dollar store, a yummy treat, or simply taking the evening off for some quiet time.

Display a nativity scene in a main room of your home. Give each of your children a figurine of one of the Wise Men. Set the figures at the entryway to the room. Each day, discuss how the children were obedient that day and move the Wise Men forward a step for each time the children were obedient. Continue until the Wise Men reach the nativity scene. Celebrate your children's obedience and thank them for choosing to be "wise" men!

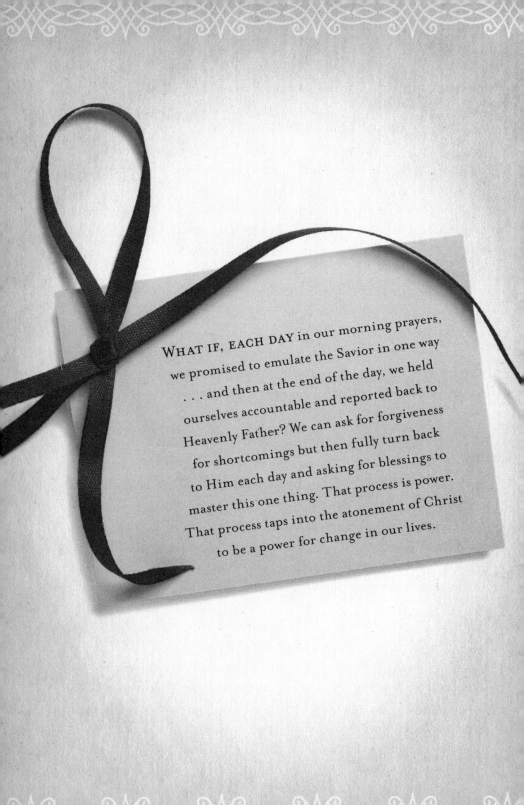

WHAT IF, EACH DAY in our morning prayers, we promised to emulate the Savior in one way . . . and then at the end of the day, we held ourselves accountable and reported back to Heavenly Father? We can ask for forgiveness for shortcomings but then fully turn back to Him each day and asking for blessings to master this one thing. That process is power. That process taps into the atonement of Christ to be a power for change in our lives.

CHAPTER 6

The Gift of Emulation

We have four sons. I have to admit that was a shock for me. I was the fourth daughter in my family and had only one younger brother; I didn't know what to do with boys.

As I learned to be a mother to my sons, one thing became very clear: little boys want to be like their dad.

It started when my boys were very young. They loved to wear Dad's T-shirts as jammies. It was a big deal when Dad would bestow one of his T-shirts on one of the boys. They would run all over the house, thrilled to be able to say, "Look, I look like Dad!"

I remember when Brennan was three years old, standing by Dad's bedside early on Saturday mornings. Brennan, who was a morning person, would energetically tap on his dad's shoulder, who was definitely *not* a morning person. "Dad, get up! Get up! We need to go work!" Brennan loved "working" alongside his dad around the house.

As my boys grew older, they all became Boy Scouts, and their dad was always nearby as their Scoutmaster. I would watch them as they "geared up" with their dad, putting on their backpacks and camping paraphernalia, ready to tackle the mountain.

My sons are all young adults now, and I see them sitting together with their laptops, discussing technology like others discuss football. Even now, they are becoming like their dad in many ways that they don't even realize.

And I see our oldest son with his little boy. I see the same patience, the same gentleness, the same efforts to teach his son that my son experienced with his dad.

A chip off the old block.

Emulation. To become like Him.

At Christmastime, we think of the baby Jesus. He came here to become like His Father and to perfectly do the will of the Father. Jesus states, "Behold I have given unto you my gospel, and this is the gospel which I have given unto you—that I came into the world to do the will of my Father, because my Father sent me" (3 Nephi 27:13). He came to atone for us so that it would finally, miraculously, be possible for us to overcome our mortality and become like our Heavenly Father.

Our Heavenly Father sent His Son to us, and Christ has repeatedly instructed and encouraged us that we are to become like Him: "Therefore I would that ye should be perfect even as I, or your Father who is in heaven is perfect" (3 Nephi 12:48). This is the desire of our hearts and the goal of our lives.

President George Q. Cannon put it beautifully:

> There was a period when we, with Jesus and others, basked in the light of the presence of God and enjoyed His smiles. We are the children of God, and as His children there is no attribute we ascribe to Him that we do not possess, though they may be dormant or in embryo. The mission of the Gospel is to develop these powers and make us like our Heavenly Parent. (*Gospel Truth: Discourses and Writings of George Q. Cannon*, sel. Jerreld L. Newquist [Salt Lake City: Deseret Book: 1974], 3)

So we begin, step by step, just as our Savior did:

> And I, John, saw that he received not of the fulness at the first, but received grace for grace;
> And he received not of the fulness at first, but continued from grace to grace, until he received a fulness. (Doctrine and Covenants 93:12–13)

We can begin taking those steps of growth, those first steps of emu-lation, by identifying and working on each grace—each positive attribute that is true to who we really are and who we are destined to be.

But sometimes this can be hard to do. We have to balance examining that long list of behaviors and attributes of Christ and striving to emulate them and not let the process devolve into yet another giant to-do list. How do we find our way? How do we know what we need to work on first?

Simple. We can turn to Him—the one who knows us best and what's best for us—and ask Him, "What can I do to emulate thy Son?"

We may be guided to work on one thing for five years. Or we may be prompted to focus on many attributes or behaviors throughout the year.

Through this process, it is helpful to focus on who we are becoming rather than simply checking items off our lists. Elder Dallin H. Oaks gives us great counsel on becoming: "In contrast to the institutions of the world, which teach us to *know* something, the gospel of Jesus Christ challenges us to *become* something" ("The Challenge to Become," *Ensign,* November 2000, 32; emphasis in original).

Indeed, the gospel of Jesus Christ challenges us to become like Him. We are challenged to become celestial beings, filled with light and love and goodness.

Elder Oaks also counseled us on this great desire to become:

> To achieve our eternal destiny, we will desire and work for the qualities required to become an eternal being. For example, eternal beings forgive all who have wronged them. They put the welfare of others ahead of themselves. And they love all of God's children. If this seems too difficult—and surely it is not easy for any of us—then we should begin with a desire for such qualities and call upon our loving Heavenly Father for help with our feelings. ("Desire," *Ensign,* May 2011, 44–45)

We begin with the desire, and then we strive to become. Throughout this effort, remember that we can turn to and count on our loving

Redeemer to guide us and mold us as *He* would, not as we would. We are never alone in this process.

It is also critical to remember that the only comparison needed is comparing ourselves to the Lord—that is all. We need not, nor should not, compare ourselves to others. It is certainly good to be inspired by the goodness of others, and we can learn from others as well, but we need not compare our progress against theirs, for we truly never know what they are dealing with and it is almost always different from what we are experiencing.

Our covenants help us in this process of *becoming*. Our covenants and the ordinances of the gospel teach us holiness and godliness. In other words, they teach us how to be godlike. They teach us how to emulate Him.

Our baptism and our partaking of the sacrament weekly is a perfect example. We are asked to covenant to "always remember Him" (Doctrine and Covenants 20:77). Why? I believe it is in part so that we will choose to *be like* Him. When tempted, we will remember Him and choose a godlike response. When the world creeps in, we will remember Him and choose to make Him a priority. Always remembering Him means that we are constantly trying to emulate Him, and we can grow more holy and more godlike in the process.

Our temple covenants include covenants where we receive clear instructions on how to become more holy and how to make our behavior more godlike. The blessings offered in the temple are portents of things to come as we strive to become more like our Savior. The temple sealing ordinance also offers marvelous promises to us that we will be successful in becoming like our Savior and living an eternal life like His.

We can use the power of covenants in our lives to be accountable to God for our progress. Sacrament meeting can take on new meaning for us as we renew our covenant, taking a moment to spiritually and privately report on our progress of our individual efforts to become like the Savior.

But such reflection doesn't have to happen only on Sunday. What if, each day in our morning prayers, we promised to emulate the Savior in some way . . . and then at the end of the day, we held ourselves accountable and reported back to Heavenly Father on how we did? If we achieved our goal, it would be a beautiful moment to rejoice with Him on our success. If not, we can ask for His forgiveness for our shortcomings and then plead for help to do better tomorrow.

That is how we become better and how we become more like the Savior.

That process is power. That process taps into the atonement of Christ and becomes a power for change in our lives.

Mormon shares with us his vision of who we can become:

> Wherefore, my beloved brethren, pray unto the Father with all the energy of heart, that ye may be filled with this love, which he hath bestowed upon all who are true followers of his Son, Jesus Christ; that ye may become the sons of God; that when he shall appear we shall be like him, for we shall see him as he is; that we may have this hope; that we may be purified even as he is pure. (Moroni 7:48)

Emulation. That we shall be like Him. This is our prayer and our gift.

We can give our Savior the gift of emulation. He has asked us to come unto Him, to learn of Him, and to be like Him. Each day we can make that choice to answer His call and give Him this great gift of emulation.

 ## Personal Scripture Study

Read Doctrine and Covenants 76 and look for ways we can become like the Savior.

 ## Family Devotional

Have each family member read a favorite verse or story from the Gospels—Matthew, Mark, Luke, or John—and discuss what they have learned about Jesus. Then ask, "What can *we* do to be like Jesus?"

As a family, discuss how you can incorporate a Christlike attribute or behavior into your daily lives. Make a list of the attributes your family would like to focus on. Write each attribute on a large piece of paper and each day (or week or month, as desired) post the paper where the whole family can see it (perhaps in the kitchen) and be reminded of the goal to be more like the Savior.

 Family Home Evening

Song: "I'm Trying to Be like Jesus," in *Children's Songbook* (Salt Lake City: The Church of Jesus Christ of Latter-day Saints, 1989), 78.

Story: "Blessed by Example"

I first came to the United States from American Samoa when I was 10 because my father wanted his children to have more educational opportunities than those he had. I lived in Seattle, Washington, with an aunt and uncle. At 14, I moved to California. My grandmother, with whom I lived, was a temple worker in the Los Angeles California Temple, but I was not a member of the Church.

During my junior year of high school, I became involved with student government and noticed several people on the student council who stood out from all the rest. They were respectful of others, clean in speech and dress, and had a dignity and light about them that caught my attention. We became friends, and they invited me to go to Mutual with them. I liked the fun, wholesome activities and the Spirit that I felt there, so I began attending regularly. Just a few weeks later my friends introduced me to the missionaries and to the Book of Mormon. I was baptized soon afterward and began a lifelong study of the Book of Mormon. (O. Vincent Haleck, "Blessed by Example," *New Era*, September 2012, 39)

Discuss how Elder Haleck was blessed by choosing to emulate his friends' good behavior and how emulating the Savior can bless our lives.

Game: The Copycat Game

The first player performs an action and then announces what they are doing: for example, clap your hands and say "I am clapping my hands!" The second player repeats the action and then announces a new action: "I am clapping my hands and I am bobbing my head." The third player must repeat *both* actions and add a third. Whoever makes a mistake gets a letter (for example, C for *cat*); the first player to spell the word is out.

For a Christmas twist, have all the actions be Christmas related: "I am smacking my lips for Christmas pie!" or "I am hanging ornaments on the tree." Also, choose a Christmas word to spell such as "star" or "Santa."

Activity: "I Can Be like Jesus"

Purchase or gather inexpensive mirrors that are large enough for each person to see their whole face. (Often dollar stores carry a good selection.) Tape or glue small pictures of Jesus around the edge of the mirror. Using permanent markers, have family members write along the bottom or the top of each mirror, "I Can Be like Jesus." Hang the mirrors in each family member's room in a prominent location where they can see the pictures every day and read the words out loud.

JUST FOR CHRISTMAS!

In a journal or a Christmas notebook begin a "Christlike" list. As you ponder, pray, and study your scriptures, write down the behaviors and attributes of Christ. How did He act? What was He like?

Choose one of Christ's attributes to emulate and focus on for a day or a week. Write the attribute and your goal on a Christmas card and display it where you will see it every day as a reminder.

Have the family discuss Christ's behaviors and attributes, and together choose one for the entire family to emulate. Select an alphabet letter ornament to represent this attribute—for example, "K" for "kindness." (You could also write the letter or the attribute on a plain ball ornament.) Hang the ornament in a prominent location to remind the family of your goal.

JESUS LOVES EACH OF US so much that any and all of our efforts to help one of His brothers or sisters is truly a gift to Him—a much-appreciated gift!

We can give that gift to Him. We can choose to see, choose to feel, and choose to reach out in love and kindness to those around us.

CHAPTER 7

The Gift of Charity

Christmas is a time of year when we turn our hearts and our lives to service. It is a natural progression from remembering Jesus to remembering His work.

I have fond memories of service at Christmastime. When I was about ten years old, my dad came home from work one day and told us about a man who worked for him. The man's son had been diagnosed with a serious condition that impacted his motor skills. My dad had asked the man what his son needed, and the man said that the doctors had told him to have his son work on his gross motor skills as much as possible—climbing, stretching, and so forth.

It sounded like a simple request, but it was wintertime in Detroit, Michigan, so it was more of a challenge. Dad asked our whole family to brainstorm ideas of what we could do to help this little boy.

Soon we came up with a plan. My dad would get some large drums and large cardboard tubes from work, and we would paint and decorate them with our favorite cartoon characters. We spent hours and hours painstakingly painting, but we were having so much fun!

The day came when the drums and tubes were finally finished. Mom got some big, red ribbon, and we tied everything together with a giant red bow. Off we went to deliver the gifts.

We drove to the family's house and quietly put the gifts on the porch. My brother rang the doorbell and we ran. We raced to the car where my parents were waiting and sat quietly in the dark with the windows rolled down slightly.

I will never forget hearing the squeals and screams of joy as the little boy and his parents discovered the giant "toys" on their porch along with a note from Santa that they were for the boy to climb on. The parents looked around carefully but did not discover us.

That evening happened more than forty years ago, but I can still picture that moment as if it had happened yesterday. I had never felt such an amazing sense of happiness and fulfillment through charity as I felt at that time.

Through the years, our family has continued a tradition of offering service at Christmastime. I have wonderful memories of my children collecting money from the neighbors and then going to buy a bicycle for a child in need. I have memories of the whole family shopping and wrapping gifts for a needy family. These memories and more warm my heart.

I also remember receiving service at this time. I remember my first year at college when I was eagerly looking forward to going home for the holidays after the semester finals. I had to help clean my apartment thoroughly to pass the dreaded inspection before I could leave though. There was a knock at the door and my visiting teacher stood there.

"I'm here to clean!" she said.

"What?" I sputtered in surprise.

She was a young college student like me and had come to help me clean so I could go home for Christmas. It was such a sweet gift of time that I remember it to this day.

I remember my Beehive class coming to my home and decorating our Christmas tree when I was grievously sick with a pregnancy. I lay on the couch and watched those sweet young women do something that brought me such joy. That tree was covered in love.

I remember a gift I received *after* Christmas one year as well. I had just endured my second round of chemotherapy for breast cancer and had lost my hair. I was sick and bald and melancholy because Christmastime was over. My sister and her husband stopped by my house on the way home from their vacation and offered to help. They packed up all my Christmas decorations—boxes and boxes of them—and helped me pull the house back together. As I sat in my chair, I was overwhelmed with their love.

Giving and receiving love is a beautiful part of Christmas. It is in honor of our Savior, the light and love of the world, that we serve.

He tells us, "Verily, verily, I say unto you, this is my gospel; and ye know the things that ye must do in my church; for the works which ye have seen me do that shall ye also do; for that which ye have seen me do even that shall ye do" (3 Nephi 27:21).

He invites us all to be part of *His* work. And His work is love.

We don't always have to do some major service project or ongoing volunteer service, though those are wonderful choices. But we can simply commit our lives to His work every day. Service can be a way of life; it can become how we live.

We can see as He sees. It is often at Christmastime when we open up our eyes to see the needs around us, but what if we committed to *see* all year long? Imagine looking at every man, woman, teenager, senior, and baby with eyes of love. If we see as He sees, we can see the great worth of a soul. We can see someone for whom He was filled with love and compassion and for whom He was willing to suffer.

We can feel as He feels. He feels love, kindness, compassion, patience, and more. We can choose to react to those around us with His feelings. We can encourage those same loving feelings to well up in our hearts continually.

We can reach out as He reaches out. The scriptures are full of stories of Christ reaching out: He reaches out to touch the eyes of the blind; He reaches out to raise the young girl back to life; He reaches out to hail His friends; He reaches out to touch the untouchable leper.

He reaches out to each one of us, continually.

We can reach out. We can say thanks for the kind word spoken to us. We can reach out and hug a person in need. We can reach out across the miles to our parents or grandparents. We can reach out to the homeless man who roams our city's streets.

We can give. Oh, we have so much we can give! Our time. Our extra change. We can give a smile or a word of encouragement. We can give hope. We can give love.

It does not take much. Truly, when Christ tells us that His yoke is easy and His burden light (Matthew 11:30), He means it. Giving love is easy, and as we extend love to others, our burdens become so very much lighter in the process.

There is a famous painting by Carl H. Bloch entitled *Healing at the Pool of Bethesda.* The image depicts several individuals standing by the pool, waiting to be healed by the waters. Christ and His Apostles are standing to the left side of the painting, and in the center is the most decrepit, tragic figure of a man beneath an awning. It is interesting to look at this painting and realize that everyone is looking away from this man, including the disciples.

But not Jesus. He approaches the man. He sees him. He even reaches out to lift the awning so that He may see him better. A pale light appears on the man's upturned face as the Savior looks upon him. And he is healed.

We can give the gift of charity to Jesus. But how does blessing the lives of others become a blessing to Him?

One day I was on my prayer walk. (I like to take a long walk each morning and pray as I do.) On this particular day I was praying for my son who had recently moved to Utah and was struggling. He was having a hard time finding good work and good friends. He was struggling with being on his own and was even questioning the values he had been taught as a child. I prayed for him mightily that day.

I thought to myself, "If anyone wanted to give something to me, it would be to help my son. That is all I want. I just want somebody, anybody, to help my son."

I prayed desperately, hoping that my son's bishop, or perhaps a home teacher, or an extended family member would reach out and help him in his time of need. And that help would be a tremendous blessing and gift to me.

Suddenly, I understood how charity can be a gift to the Savior. Our service to each other is what He wants as well! Jesus loves each of us so much that any and all of our efforts to help one of His brothers or sisters is truly a gift to Him—a much-appreciated gift!

We can give that gift to Him. We can choose to see, choose to feel, and choose to reach out in love and kindness to those around us. We can do the works that He does.

 ## Personal Scripture Study

Read 3 Nephi 17 and ponder Christ's love for the people.

 ## Family Devotional

Read and discuss the parable of the Good Samaritan found in Luke 10:25–37. Talk about what we can do to extend love to those in need. Review the miracles performed by Jesus to better understand His constant focus on those in need.

 ## Family Home Evening

Song: "Love One Another," in *Hymns of The Church of Jesus Christ of Latter-day Saints* (Salt Lake City: The Church of Jesus Christ of Latter-day Saints, 1985), no. 308, or "Once within a Lowly Stable," in *Children's Songbook* (Salt Lake City: The Church of Jesus Christ of Latter-day Saints, 1989), 41.

Story: Invite family members to share experiences when they either received service from someone else or when they gave service to someone. Talk about how giving and receiving service makes you feel. Also discuss the times the family did service together and the blessings that came from it.

Game: Service Sniper

Write down a list of twelve service projects you could do for your neighbors (outside activities only). The list could include such projects as shoveling snow, raking leaves, weeding a flowerbed, washing a window, writing "hello" in colored chalk on their driveway, singing Christmas carols, making a snowman, or hanging a candy cane on their door. Number your list. Gather a pair of dice and any supplies that might be needed.

At each house, roll the dice and do the service project that matches the number!

Activity: Angel Scavenger Hunt

For this activity, you will be gathering food items from around your neighborhood to create a meal for a family in need.

Begin by writing down a list of items needed for the meal: cans of vegetables, a box of stuffing, a cake mix, and so forth (emphasize nonperishables). Then gather several grocery bags and go to the homes in your neighborhood. Ask your neighbors to contribute one item on your list (or more if they're feeling generous).

After all the food has been gathered, take the full grocery bags to the family in need. Put it on the porch, ring the doorbell, and run!

A parent could stay close to the house to make sure the family is home and picks up the food—but be careful and don't get caught!

(This activity is also fun if the whole family dresses up like angels.)

Just for Christmas!

 Choose a Christmas service project to do as an individual or as a family. Here are some ideas:

- Tie a quilt for a family in need in your neighborhood, or donate it to the LDS Humanitarian Center. To tie a quilt, place a layer of batting between two pieces of fabric and tie with yarn. Sew the ends together. Another easy blanket can be made using two large rectangles of fleece material. Cut the ends into two-inch strips (like wide fringe) and tie the two strips together with square knots.
- Take up a collection throughout your neighborhood, your work, or your school. Donate the proceeds to your local children's charity.
- Collect your change all month long (or all year long!) and donate the money to someone in need.

- Serve at the local food bank or soup kitchen. (Check with your county for locations near your neighborhood.)
- Make sack lunches and take them to the homeless. Be sure and include a Christmas treat!
- Make a gift basket for a person who is lonely or suffering. Go to the dollar store and have each family member pick out an item. Come home and wrap each gift. Add treats to the basket and deliver the present. Remember: the visit is just as important as the treat!
- Start "An Angel in the Neighborhood" program. Perform an anonymous service for a neighbor and then post a picture of an angel on your neighbor's door. Give them an extra copy of the angel picture— one to keep and one to share—along with the following poem:

> *An Angel flew by*
> *And came to our door.*
> *Singing "Good tidings to all!*
> *The needy and the poor."*
>
> *So we've done a good deed*
> *But no one will know.*
> *Now it's your turn to join in*
> *So caring will flow.*
>
> *Just do one kindly act*
> *To anyone in need.*
> *Then fly this Angel and poem*
> *To another's door to read.*

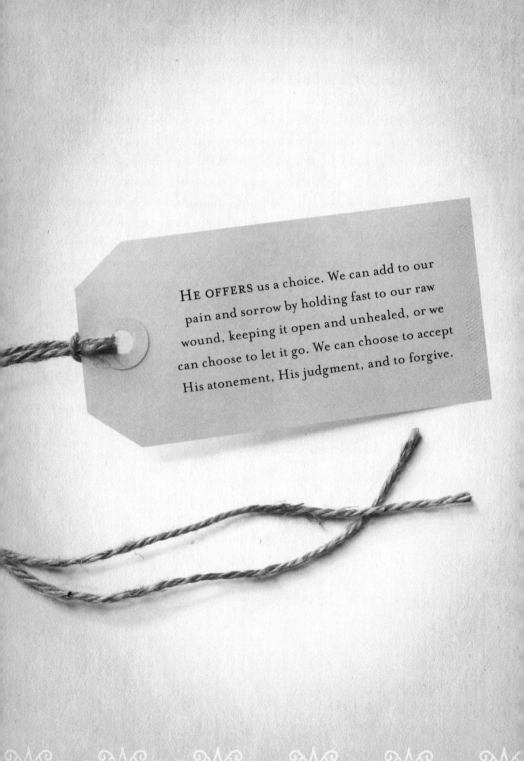

He OFFERS us a choice. We can add to our pain and sorrow by holding fast to our raw wound, keeping it open and unhealed, or we can choose to let it go. We can choose to accept His atonement, His judgment, and to forgive.

CHAPTER 8

The Gift of Forgiveness

One of my favorite parts of the Christmas story is actually a part that is often skimmed over, but one that should not be missed. The story tells of the understanding heart of the man who would help raise the Son of God on earth.

In Matthew 1, we read that Mary "was found with child" (Matthew 1:18). Such news was a deep shock to Joseph, who knew the baby was not his. How did he react?

The scriptures tell us: "Then Joseph her husband, being a just man, and not willing to make a publick example, was minded to put her away privily" (Matthew 1:19).

Joseph was a just man. He was a man of fairness and wisdom. He was not someone to react with anger or rage.

And as Joseph pondered the situation, he decided not to make a public spectacle of Mary.

Think about that. Such a decision speaks volumes of the character of this man. Mary's reputation was on the line—but so was Joseph's. He could have demanded an open, public formality that would have placed all the blame and all the shame squarely on Mary's shoulders and also relieved himself of any responsibility. He didn't want to do that.

Joseph loved Mary. He decided he would handle things privately to protect her as much as he could.

Then as Joseph pondered his decision, he received a visit from the angel of the Lord, who told him the truth of the situation.

But never forget, even before Joseph knew the whole story, he had chosen the path of love and understanding.

We have all been hurt in our lives. We all have experienced the pain, the resentment, and the aches that come from bumping up against each other along this path of mortality. Some wounds run very deep and are very raw. Some pain is unjustified and undeserved.

Christ knows all about pain. He suffered greatly throughout His life. He was rejected by His friends and neighbors and fellow church members. He endured unrelenting attacks by Satan. He faced betrayal. He was crucified. He understands what it's like to be hurt.

And He offers us a choice. We can add to our pain and sorrow by holding onto our raw wound, keeping it open and unhealed, or we can choose to let the pain go. We can choose to accept His atonement, His judgment, and to forgive.

The choice can be a difficult one. Some hurts go beyond description. Many, if not most, happen without our fault. And in many situations, if not most, the person who harmed us is not asking for forgiveness.

And Jesus whispers to us the way to be healed: forgive. Forgive it all. Accept His payment, accept His healing, and forgive all.

Ponder how you can have a forgiving heart. Ponder how you can, once and for all, let go of your pain and sorrow and hand it over to Him.

Choose healing. Choose to let go. Give the Savior the gift of accepting His atonement—not only for you, but for everyone around you.

Choose to forgive.

 Personal Scripture Study

Read Mosiah 2–4 and ponder forgiveness.

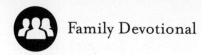

 Family Devotional

Read and discuss President Dieter F. Uchtdorf's talk, "The Merciful Obtain Mercy," *Ensign,* May 2012, 70, 75–77. Discuss how your family can be blessed by forgiveness from the Lord and how you can extend forgiveness and mercy to others.

Family Home Evening

Song: "Help Me, Dear Father," in *Children's Songbook* (Salt Lake City: The Church of Jesus Christ of Latter-day Saints, 1989), 99, or "Hark! the Herald Angels Sing," in *Hymns of The Church of Jesus Christ of Latter-day Saints* (Salt Lake City: The Church of Jesus Christ of Latter-day Saints, 1985), no. 209.

Story: Review the following scriptures: Matthew 12; Mark 14; Luke 13; 22; 23; and John 5; 7. Discuss how Jesus was mistreated during His mortal life and how He forgave freely.

Game: I Forgive You!

Each family member is given ten game pieces (you can use pennies or buttons). Vary the number of game pieces depending on the age of the children and how fast you want the game to go.

On individual index cards, write down the following colors: red, yellow, blue, white, green, purple, black, brown, and orange. On two cards, write the words "I forgive you!" Shuffle the cards together and put them face-down in the middle of the game area.

The first player chooses a card and shows it to the others. Anyone who is wearing the color listed on the card gives one of their pieces to the person holding the card. Then the next player chooses a card.

If the player selects an "I forgive you!" card, that player gives one of their pieces to each of the other players. Each person then says, "Oh, thank you, so much!" and gives the player a big kiss.

The player who gets rid of all their pieces first wins.

Activity: That's OK!

Have the children practice saying "That's OK!" For small children, teach them to sign "OK" with their fingers by making an "O" with the thumb and first finger and spreading the other fingers straight up.

As a family, discuss how it is a blessing to forgive others and how forgiveness can bless the family. All week long, when there is contention or stress in the family, stop and call out "That's OK!" Repeat as necessary!

JUST FOR CHRISTMAS!

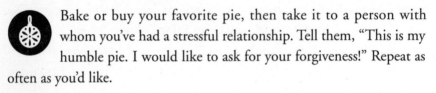 Bake or buy your favorite pie, then take it to a person with whom you've had a stressful relationship. Tell them, "This is my humble pie. I would like to ask for your forgiveness!" Repeat as often as you'd like.

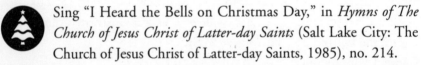 Sing "I Heard the Bells on Christmas Day," in *Hymns of The Church of Jesus Christ of Latter-day Saints* (Salt Lake City: The Church of Jesus Christ of Latter-day Saints, 1985), no. 214.

Then read the story behind the song in the book *I Heard the Bells on Christmas Day* by Lloyd D. Newell (Salt Lake City: Deseret Book, 2009).

As a family, discuss how you can help bring "peace on earth, good will to men." Set a goal to be peacemakers in your family, your extended family, and your neighborhood. Set a goal to forgive others for the things they do that may be hurtful to you.

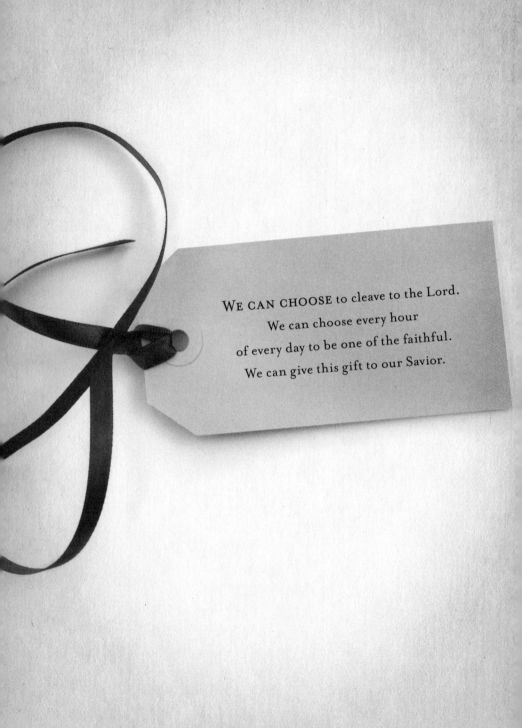

WE CAN CHOOSE to cleave to the Lord.
We can choose every hour
of every day to be one of the faithful.
We can give this gift to our Savior.

CHAPTER 9

The Gift of Faithfulness

Two people in the Christmas story deserve special attention: Simeon and Anna. Though they appear only briefly in Jesus' life story, these faithful souls were given the special privilege of being witnesses of Christ's divinity.

Joseph and Mary took Jesus to be circumcised and dedicated to the Lord at the temple and to offer sacrifice to fulfill the requirements of the law of Moses. It was there that they met Simeon:

> And, behold, there was a man in Jerusalem, whose name was Simeon; and the same man was just and devout, waiting for the consolation of Israel: and the Holy Ghost was upon him.
>
> And it was revealed unto him by the Holy Ghost, that he should not see death, before he had seen the Lord's Christ.
>
> And he came by the Spirit into the temple: and when the parents brought in the child Jesus, to do for him after the custom of the law,
>
> Then took he him up in his arms, and blessed God, and said,
>
> Lord, now lettest thou thy servant depart in peace, according to thy word:
>
> For mine eyes have seen thy salvation,
>
> Which thou hast prepared before the face of all people;

A light to lighten the Gentiles, and the glory of thy people Israel.

And Joseph and his mother marvelled at those things which were spoken of him. (Luke 2:25–33)

Simeon was a faithful man. When the Spirit prompted him to go to the temple, he went and was blessed to be a witness of the Christ child.

Then Joseph and Mary met Anna. Anna was a very old woman who was called a "prophetess" (Luke 2:36). She was a deeply devout and faithful woman whose life consisted of full-time service to the Lord; she was filled with the Holy Ghost and the spirit of revelation.

And she was a widow of about fourscore and four years, which departed not from the temple, but served God with fastings and prayers night and day.

And she coming in that instant gave thanks likewise unto the Lord, and spake of him to all them that looked for redemption in Jerusalem. (Luke 2:37–38)

A faithful man. A faithful woman. And God rewarded their lifetime of commitment by allowing them to be two witnesses of the Messiah.

Faithfulness is deeply personal. It's that steady, day in, day out commitment to serve God and be true to Him. There's nothing flashy about faithfulness. Instead, it is an internal compass that leads us on a fixed course toward our Savior.

I love these lyrics:

The soul that on Jesus hath leaned for repose
I will not, I cannot, desert to his foes;
That soul, though all hell should endeavor to shake,
I'll never, no never, I'll never, no never,
I'll never, no never, no never forsake! ("How Firm a Foundation," in *Hymns of The Church of Jesus Christ of Latter-day Saints* [Salt Lake City: The Church of Jesus Christ of Latter-day Saints, 1985], no. 85)

Elder Neil L. Andersen shares his feelings on faithfulness, saying, "Perfection does not come in this life, but we exercise faith in the Lord Jesus Christ and keep our covenants" ("Never Leave Him," *Ensign,* November 2010, 41). And President Thomas S. Monson has promised, "Your testimony, when constantly nourished, will keep you safe" ("May You Have Courage," *Ensign,* May 2009, 126).

How can we live faithful lives? In what ways can we exhibit that steady willingness to be true and faithful in all things?

We can choose to cleave to the Lord. We can choose every hour of every day to be one of the faithful. We can give this gift to our Savior.

 Personal Scripture Study

Read 3 Nephi 1:9–22 about how Nephi prayed for the faithful who believed in Christ's coming but who were about to be killed for their beliefs.

 Family Devotional

Read Mosiah 18 and discuss Alma the Elder. Talk about how he changed his ways and was thereafter completely faithful to the Lord. Discuss how his actions led many people to lives of faithfulness. Make a list of what each family member could do to be more faithful to the Lord.

 Family Home Evening

Song: "Come, Follow Me," in *Hymns of The Church of Jesus Christ of Latter-day Saints* (Salt Lake City: The Church of Jesus Christ of Latter-day Saints, 1985), no. 116, or "Oh, Come, All Ye Faithful," in *Hymns,* no. 202.

Story: Share stories of individuals from your family history who demonstrated their faithfulness to the Savior.

Game: Faithful Freddie

Players gather in a circle, each one wearing a hat of some kind. Hardboil an egg (or use a plastic Easter egg).

Announce to the family that Freddie is always faithful and takes care of his egg. The first player stands in the circle and closes his or her eyes. One of the other players is "Faithful Freddie" and puts the egg under his or her hat.

The first player opens his or her eyes and then asks each person in the circle, "Are you Faithful Freddie?" The player can stare into their eyes carefully or look them over but cannot touch their hat. Each player tries to keep a straight face—especially Freddie!

After the player has questioned everyone, he or she must make a guess as to who has the hidden egg. If the player is correct, he or she gets one point. If the player is incorrect, the point is awarded to "Freddie."

The person sitting to the right of Freddie is the next to stand in the circle. The first player to reach five points wins.

Activity: Faith and Works

As a family, do an activity to help your ward. Perhaps you could clean the church building (specifically the kitchen or bathrooms), clean around the outside of the building, repair hymnbooks, clean and organize the library, or more. Discuss with the bishop any other activity that you could do to help out your ward family.

JUST FOR CHRISTMAS!

Think about going the extra mile in your church calling for Christmas. Consider writing thank-you notes to those you work with. Perhaps you might choose to spend more time preparing to teach. Especially make an effort to connect with your visiting teaching or home teaching families. What could you do to bless their lives and help bring them to Christ? Ponder that question deeply and seek inspiration for an answer to that prayer.

Purchase some glow-in-the-dark stars and attach a star to the ceiling above each child's bed. As a family, discuss how the Wise Men were faithful in following the guidance of the Spirit and how their faithfulness helped Jesus and His family. Talk about how the Wise Men's journey was long and difficult and how, even though they were threatened by the king, they stayed true and faithful to what they knew was right.

As the children look at the star on the ceiling each night, encourage them to ponder about how they had been faithful that day.

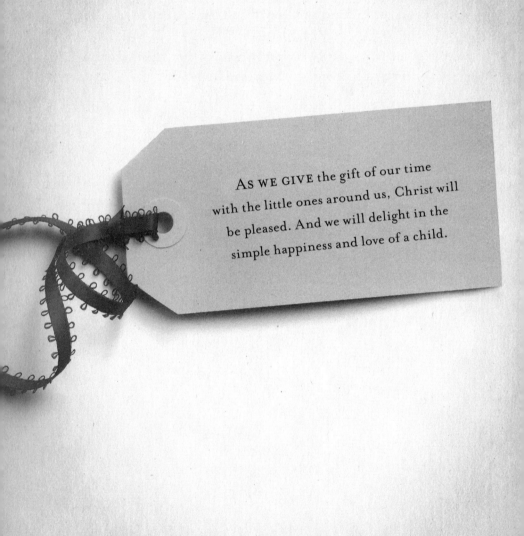

As we give the gift of our time with the little ones around us, Christ will be pleased. And we will delight in the simple happiness and love of a child.

CHAPTER 10

The Gift of Love

As an adult, my dad didn't really like little kids. He loved his own children, of course, but other children . . . well, not so much. One day, he was reading in the Book of Mormon and read the account of the resurrected Jesus appearing to the Nephites. He read of Jesus calling all the little children to Him.

> And it came to pass that he commanded that their little children should be brought.

> So they brought their little children and set them down upon the ground round about him, and Jesus stood in the midst; and the multitude gave way till they had all been brought unto him.

> And it came to pass that when they had all been brought, and Jesus stood in the midst, he commanded the multitude that they should kneel down upon the ground. . . .

> And when he had said these words, he himself also knelt upon the earth; and behold he prayed unto the Father, and the things which he prayed cannot be written, and the multitude did bear record who heard him.

> And after this manner do they bear record: The eye hath never seen, neither hath the ear heard, before, so great and marvelous things as we saw and heard Jesus speak unto the Father;

And no tongue can speak, neither can there be written by any man, neither can the hearts of men conceive so great and marvelous things as we both saw and heard Jesus speak; and no one can conceive of the joy which filled our souls at the time we heard him pray for us unto the Father. . . .

And they arose from the earth, and he said unto them: Blessed are ye because of your faith. And now behold, my joy is full.

And when he had said these words, he wept, and the multitude bare record of it, and he took their little children, one by one, and blessed them, and prayed unto the Father for them.

And when he had done this he wept again;

And he spake unto the multitude, and said unto them: Behold your little ones.

And as they looked to behold they cast their eyes towards heaven, and they saw the heavens open, and they saw angels descending out of heaven as it were in the midst of fire; and they came down and encircled those little ones about, and they were encircled about with fire; and the angels did minister unto them. (3 Nephi 17:11–13, 15–17, 20–24)

As my father read these verses, he was overcome by the love the Savior had for the little children. He was amazed that He would take each child, one by one, and bless him or her individually and pray to the Father for him or her individually. My father pondered how the Savior of the World felt about the little ones.

My dad realized he needed to change. He decided that if the Messiah considered little children to be that important to love, then he should love them too. He developed a plan.

Each week, my dad would fill his pockets with little candies. And then he would talk to each of the children at church. Soon, the children realized that Brother Browne was the Candyman! As you might imagine, he became very popular. The children loved my dad!

Soon, my dad loved the children as well. Throughout the rest of his life, he would go out of his way to talk to little children and make them feel happy and loved.

In his later years as a granddad, he would teach his grandchildren and great-grandchildren his secret wave. He would ask, "Do you know how to tell your mommy that you love her without saying a word?"

The child would stare up at this man with white hair and a big smile and shake their heads.

"Ah, let me teach you!" he would answer.

Then he would show them how to bend their index finger three times. "That means, 'I love you!'" he would explain. He delighted in teaching the little ones.

Christmas is a delightful time to be with children. They love every experience—every song, every story, every treat! As we spend time with little ones, we are reminded of the essence of life.

So make some time this Christmas season to stop, sit down, and spend time with a little one in your life. Read a book. Sing a silly song. Take a walk.

You will find, as my father did, that your life will be richly blessed. Jesus loves the little children of the world, and He wants them to be loved. As we give the gift of our time with the little ones around us, Christ will be pleased, and we will delight in the simple happiness and love of a child.

 ## Personal Scripture Study

Read Luke 18:15–17; 3 Nephi 17:11–25; 26:14–16.

 ## Family Devotional

Read Luke 18:15–17; 3 Nephi 17:11–25; 26:14–16. As a family, discuss how Jesus felt about children and how He treated them. Talk about what each of us can do to be more loving and caring toward little children.

Family Home Evening

Song: "Jesus Loved the Little Children," in *Children's Songbook* (Salt Lake City: The Church of Jesus Christ of Latter-day Saints, 1989), 59, or "Away in a Manger," in *Children's Songbook*, 42.

Story: Invite your children to share a story about another child they like or admire. Talk about how we can be like Christ when we love little children.

Game: Baby Doll Relay

Gather a baby doll and supplies for a relay. (If the family is large enough, divide into two teams.) Each participant will run up to the baby doll, perform the specified action, and then run back. The player (or team) with the fastest time wins.

- Kiss the baby!
- Put a diaper on the baby! (Allow small children to use diapers with Velcro-fasteners; older kids can use safety pins.)
- Wrap the baby in a blanket!
- Sing to the baby!
- Dance with the baby!
- Hug the baby and tell him you love him!
- Bring the baby to Mommy!

If playing this game at Christmastime, have the doll represent the baby Jesus.

Activity: Bless the Children

As a family, think of the children in need in your area and then choose a service project that will help them.

Ideas might include:

Make a Newborn Kit

Make a newborn kit and donate it to your Ward Humanitarian Leader (see http://www.ldsphilanthropies.org/humanitarian-services /latter-day-saint-humanitarian-10-8-1.html).

Birthday Cards for Foster Kids

Gather materials needed to make birthday cards (for example, blank note cards, envelopes, colored paper, cardstock, stickers, markers, crayons, glue, scissors, etc.). Talk to the family about children who live in the foster care system in your community. Brainstorm about what kinds of birthday cards these children might like.

Have a card-making night where you make birthday cards (or just "We love you!" cards) for all age groups and genders. Have the entire family sign each card. (Remember to leave the envelopes open so the foster parents can see which child the card would be appropriate for.)

Deliver the cards to your local children's foster care facility. (Call your county government if you're not familiar with the location or contact information.) If permitted, go to the facility as a family.

Welcome Baby Day

Identify a family in your ward or neighborhood who has a brand-new baby. Contact the parents and offer to bring dinner one evening.

As a family, work together to prepare a lovely dinner. (Remember to include dessert!) Make sure you make something the family will enjoy (it's OK to ask for a list of favorite foods or about any food allergies!) and that you make enough. Take the meal in disposable containers so the mother doesn't have to worry about returning dishes.

Also include with your dinner basket a small toy, blanket, book, or other gift to be given to the new baby from your family. You can make the gift or have the children help you select something from the store. If there is only one other child in the family, such as a toddler, it might be wise to bring the older sibling a small gift as well, like a ball or bubbles.

As a family, deliver the dinner and the small gift. Have a nice visit with the family where you admire the baby and congratulate them. A short visit is pleasant. Enjoy the new baby!

(Other service ideas can be found in Merrilee Boyack, *52 Weeks of Fun Family Service* [Salt Lake City: Deseret Book, 2007].)

Just for Christmas!

Contact your local children's hospital, children's home, or preschool. Ask what help they need and how you can help the children. It may be to visit, collect books, or help a specific child in need.

If a donation on the local level is not possible, participate in the "Toys for Tots" program. (Visit toysfortots.org for more information.)

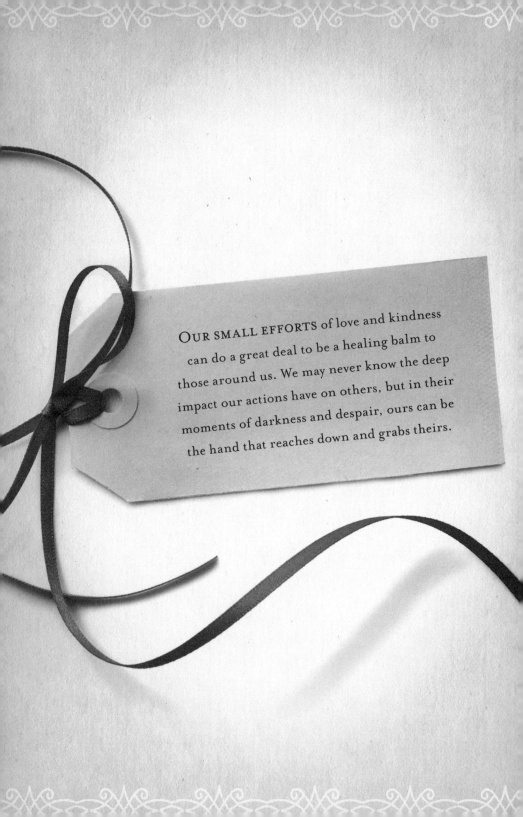

OUR SMALL EFFORTS of love and kindness can do a great deal to be a healing balm to those around us. We may never know the deep impact our actions have on others, but in their moments of darkness and despair, ours can be the hand that reaches down and grabs theirs.

CHAPTER 11

The Gift of a Healing Balm

It was a few weeks before Christmas. Our California community was still reeling from the wildfires that had swept through and burned hundreds of homes to the ground. My sister Kathe had organized a community-wide holiday boutique for the devastated families. Thousands of items had been donated—some homemade, some brand-new, and some lovingly shared.

I sat at the tables checking in the families who had lost everything. I shall never forget one family I met that day. Lisa (her name has been changed to protect her privacy) approached the table with her husband and their little family. Bandages covered one of her eyes; she explained that she was suffering from a serious eye condition.

She shared a bit of their story with me. Her husband had lost his job, and the fires had swept through and destroyed everything they had. They did not have renter's insurance and were barely surviving. Her three little ones looked up at me with the most tired, sad eyes I had ever seen in children.

I invited them in to the boutique, gave them a big box, and told them to take anything they wanted. Her husband straightened up his shoulders, and the children beamed as they looked in on what appeared to be a fairyland.

But I was shaken. I couldn't imagine the suffering this little family had endured. I resolved that this family needed some human angels.

I sent out an e-mail that day calling for angels far and wide to respond and help this family. I have never, ever seen such an outpouring of charity in my life. In just a few days, my porch and driveway were teeming with donations. Money and gift cards poured in. I spent a lot of time at Walmart (who generously was offering us a discount) and shopped and shopped.

And then the day of magic came. We drove up in a moving van to this family's new little rental house and love just poured out of that van. New beds, couches, dishes, bedspreads—you name it.

After we got everything moved in, the children came back home. We had completely furnished an entire house from head to toe—including a Christmas tree with wrapped gifts beneath it. It was a miracle like nothing I'd ever seen. Hundreds of people had participated to give love to this family and to help relieve their suffering.

Suffering is all around us. It can be from a big tragedy such as what happened to Lisa's family. Or it can be something small and unseen—a lonely young woman at Church who feels unnoticed and unloved.

Every effort we make to relieve suffering increases light and love in this world. Imagine how Jesus feels when we offer a healing balm to relieve the suffering of those He loves.

I remember once having a painful medical procedure that lasted quite a long time. I shall never forget the nurse who reached over and just held my hand, patting it reassuringly. That small gesture of love so greatly relieved my suffering that, to this day, the thought of it makes me weep.

Our small efforts of love and kindness can do a great deal to be a healing balm to those around us. We may never know the deep impact our actions have on others, but in their moments of darkness and despair, ours can be the hand that reaches down and grabs theirs.

This gift of compassion is one of the Savior's most treasured gifts. He sees our reaching out. He sees our efforts of love. He loves our loving.

So who is suffering around you? Who is lonely or afraid or sick or in despair? What small gesture can you make to relieve their suffering for a brief moment? How can you reach out your hand to them?

As we ponder this gift to our Savior, we can share with those around us the healing love that has been given to us by Him. Our gift to Him is to be His hands.

Personal Scripture Study

Read Matthew 11 and note all the efforts to relieve suffering.

Family Devotional

Read Matthew 25 and discuss each of the parables. As a family, discuss how you can follow the direction of the Savior to relieve suffering.

Family Home Evening

Song: "I Think When I Read That Sweet Story," in *Children's Songbook* (Salt Lake City: The Church of Jesus Christ of Latter-day Saints, 1989), 56, or "Silent Night," in *Hymns of The Church of Jesus Christ of Latter-day Saints* (Salt Lake City: The Church of Jesus Christ of Latter-day Saints, 1985), no. 204.

Story: Salea Is Healed

Maria sat down and carefully lowered her young daughter next to her on the bench. "There you go, Salea. Just let Mommy rest for a moment."

Young Salea reached out and patted her mother's arm. The young girl had been blind from birth. All her life her mother had carried Salea on her back. She had done everything for her—including saving her life. When the darkness had come and the earthquakes had hit their city, their home collapsed and Salea's mother had grabbed her and run to safety. Salea adored her mother.

"We're almost there," said Maria, "almost there." Wearily, she picked up her daughter and swung her around on her back. "Here we go!" she said. She started walking down the path toward the large temple in the distance. "The prophets have told us that Jesus will come. Let's hope he will come to the temple," she said.

The mother and daughter reached the temple and sat on the lower step. All was quiet.

"Let's pray, Mother," said Salea.

"Good idea," said Maria. They held hands and prayed together quietly. The day passed and evening came. Mother and daughter made themselves as comfortable as they could to sleep. The next morning many people began gathering to worship.

After a time, all was quiet. "Can you hear that, Mother?" said Salea urgently.

"Hear what?" said Maria.

"Listen! There it is again!" said the young girl.

"What do you hear?" asked her mother. And then she heard a voice speaking the words, "Behold my Beloved Son, in whom I am well pleased, in whom I have glorified my name— hear ye Him."

"Salea! There's a light up in the sky!" cried Maria. "It's a man!" Maria watched as Jesus descended from the sky and stood among the people at the temple. She told Salea everything she saw and her daughter listened intently to all that Jesus said. She was thrilled as she listened to His marvelous teachings.

When He paused and called for any sick or afflicted to be brought forward, Maria quickly scooped up Salea in her arms and pressed forward. She reached the Savior. "Please, Master. My daughter has been blind since birth. Will you heal her?"

Jesus reached out His hands and touched Salea's eyes and turned her face toward her mother.

Salea looked up and saw light for the first time. She blinked several times and then opened her eyes wide and saw her mother for the first time in her life. "Mother!" she exclaimed.

"Oh, Salea, you can see!" Her mother hugged her tightly.

"I can see! I can see!" exclaimed Salea.

Maria turned back to Jesus. "Oh, thank you, thank you so much!" she cried as she fell at His feet.

Jesus reached out to her, lifting her. Great strength and healing poured through Maria. She felt the Savior's love wash over her, healing her hurts and sadness. She was filled with joy. "You are the beloved of God!" she exclaimed.

Salea and her mother knew that Jesus was the source of hope and healing. And they were grateful.

Game: "We're Helping!" Pair Charades

Write the following list of activities on individual slips of paper. Collect them in a hat or small box.

- Helping an old lady cross the road
- Visiting a sick person in the hospital
- Helping a child carry a heavy package
- Helping a blind person cross the room
- Feeding a hungry person
- Visiting a lonely person
- Pulling weeds for a grandpa
- Cleaning windows for a grandma
- Giving clothes to a needy person
- Giving money to a homeless person
- Helping a person in a wheelchair go shopping
- Shoveling snow (or raking leaves or sweeping) for a single mom
- Inviting a single dad over for dinner
- Writing a letter to a military person
- Giving a ride to a family without a car

- Shaking hands with a new person at church or school
- Sitting by a person who needs a friend
- Helping a mom with a new baby
- Hugging a sad person

Divide up into pairs (a team of three is OK if you have uneven numbers). Have each pair pick a slip of paper from the hat and act out the scene without using any words. The other family members must guess how they're helping.

Activity: Visit the Lonely

Organize a visit to a local nursing home or care facility. Call ahead of time to discuss what the residents would like most. Have the children color pictures or make Christmas items or cards to decorate and take with them. Remind the children that what the grandmas and grandpas want most is company! (Bringing candy or food treats is usually not a good idea due to dietary restrictions.)

You can prepare your children by talking about what to expect during a visit. Many seniors would be delighted to hear the children talk about what they are doing to prepare for Christmas and would love to hear them sing. Rather than a group presentation, consider going into their rooms and chatting with them individually. Remind the children that even if the people they visit can't talk or acknowledge them, their spirits know that they're there and they're so happy!

If your children are very young, a visit to a nursing home may be daunting. Instead, visit a senior in your neighborhood or ward.

Just for Christmas!

Ponder and pray about the people around you who might be suffering or in need of aid. Become a living "shepherd" to them as prompted. As you extend service to those in need, you could hang a candy cane on your tree to remind you of the Good Shepherd.

Participate in a Twinkle Star project. Every day have each family member promise to "twinkle." They can smile or wave at a stranger or give someone a compliment.

Cut out a large star and put it on your refrigerator. Then get a package of star stickers. At dinner, invite family members to share what they did that day to "twinkle." For every act of service, add a small star sticker to the big star.

JOY COMES in all forms of living. But it mostly comes in small things and in small ways. Throughout the coming week, grab hold of those little joyful moments.

CHAPTER 12

The Gift of Joy

It was a sweet little video. It was evening and my son and his little family were driving home. His oldest son, Keaton, was three and had learned to sing all three verses of "Silent Night." And in the soft glow of the evening, my son recorded little Keaton singing for all he was worth—"Silent night! Holy night! All is calm, all is bright." On and on he sang.

Such beautiful joy radiated from his little face as he sang of the Savior—his Savior. In the hustle and bustle of the season, that little video of that sweet child singing of Jesus was a moment of joy—pure joy.

Mortality is not an easy experience. But every day we are faced with a choice. We can choose to live with misery or we can choose to live with joy!

Joyful people radiate a light and an energy that draws us in. My friend Betty is such a person. She has served multiple missions for her church teaching the Eskimos of Alaska about Jesus. She radiates joy. It's impossible not to smile when she is around.

Children love to live with joy. Many experiences are a delight to them—whether it's the new snow on the ground or a cool bug they've discovered. Life just bubbles up within them and beams out to those around them.

Elder Quentin L. Cook tells of a woman sharing the joy of children:

> I find it interesting that our best member missionaries, those who take the opportunity of sharing the gospel, are often people who are joyful. When I was the Executive Director of the Missionary Department, we suddenly noticed some

baptisms in France. Thrilled, we wondered about the reasons, and there were several. But one of the main reasons was a sister who went to work on Monday morning and talked about Sunbeams. After the Sabbath, she would—with great joy and delight—tell her co-workers about her experience teaching young children the day before. Before long, her associates could hardly wait for her to talk about the Sunbeams. . . .

If we rejoice in what we have, if we feel joy and express it, we are happier. We do what the Lord wants us to do, we become better people, and by association, those around us—our children and friends and neighbors—are happier. Joy is the key. ("Sunbeams, Public Affairs, and Gospel Joy," *Ensign,* December 2012, 80)

Living life with joy is a conscious choice. Ask yourself: How can I feel joyful today? What can I do to be happy and have fun and joy? Who or what can I invite into my life to have more joy? How can I spread joy to those around me? What glorious questions to ponder!

For some, joy comes in the morning when we step outside into the sunshine and fresh air. For others, joy comes from listening to a wonderful Bach flute concerto. And for still others, joy comes from holding the hand of a loved one—feeling their hearts beat together.

Joy comes in all forms, but it mostly comes in small things and in small ways. Throughout the coming week, grab hold of those little joyful moments. Share them with your Savior. He delights in your happiness. Indeed, the scriptures tell us this is the very purpose of our existence: "Men are, that they might have joy" (2 Nephi 2:25).

Live with joy! Sing, dance, laugh! Warm your day with joy in your heart and your love of God.

 ### Personal Scripture Study

Read Nephi's vision of the Savior in 1 Nephi 11:9–33; 12:4–8.

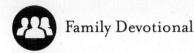 Family Devotional

Read one or more of these inspirational messages on the topic of joy and share your favorite passages with your family:

Barbara W. Winder, "Finding Joy in Life," *Ensign*, November 1987; available at www.lds.org/general-conference/1987/10/finding-joy-in-life; accessed 3 June 2013.

Thomas S. Monson, "Finding Joy in the Journey," *Ensign*, November 2008; available at www.lds.org/general-conference/2008/10/finding-joy-in -the-journey; accessed 3 June 2013.

Quentin L. Cook, "Rejoice!" *Ensign*, November 1996; available at www.lds.org/general-conference/1996/10/rejoice; accessed 3 June 2013.

Richard G. Scott, "The Path to Peace and Joy," *Ensign*, November 2000; available at www.lds.org/general-conference/2000/10/the-path-to -peace-and-joy; accessed 3 June 2013.

If your children are older, read the entire article together. Discuss how we can be joyful in our lives.

 Family Home Evening

Song: "Jesus Wants Me for a Sunbeam," in *Children's Songbook* (Salt Lake City: The Church of Jesus Christ of Latter-day Saints, 1989), 60, or "Joy to the World," in *Hymns of The Church of Jesus Christ of Latter-day Saints* (Salt Lake City: The Church of Jesus Christ of Latter-day Saints, 1985), no. 201.

Story: Toss a small item like a beanbag or ball to a family member and invite that person to share something that makes him or her feel joy. Then toss the item to another family member, who adds another story of joy.

Game: Jumping with Joy

Children follow parents around the house or yard. Parents stop in various locations and tell of a good thing that happened there. Children all jump up and down and shout, "We're jumping with joy! We're jumping with joy! Boy, oh boy, we're jumping with joy!" Then the parents lead the family to the next place in the house or yard.

Examples:

- Standing in front of a picture of parents getting married, Dad could quickly tell the story of getting married that day.
- Standing in kitchen, Mom could tell the story of last Thanksgiving dinner with the whole family.
- Standing in the baby's nursery, Dad could tell of the day that the baby came home and how happy the family was.
- Standing in the garage, Mom could tell of driving to church each Sunday with the family.

Experiences can also be linked to Christmas activities or to Jesus. For example, standing in the yard, parents could point to the moon and stars and tell how Jesus created the earth and the sun, the moon and the stars. Or standing in front of a picture of the temple, parents could explain the temple is the House of God.

Activity: Oh, Joyful Day!

Each day for a week invite each family member to choose one joyful thing for the family to do that day. Post a paper on the refrigerator with the headline "Joyful Day!" Have each person select a day and something that will bring joy to the family. It may be to paint with finger paints, have a pizza night, go to a movie together, play a game together, sing Christmas carols around the piano, or any other joyful thing.

JUST FOR CHRISTMAS!

Make a list of activities that bring you joy such as pray, call old friends and wish them a Merry Christmas, sit by the Christmas tree, visit the temple, or listen to Christmas carols. Put each one on a slip of paper and put into a small bowl or box. Each morning, pick out one activity to do that day. You could do this for a week or longer. Feel free to add more and have joy!

Do the "12 Days of Christmas Joy" as a family:

1. Have a family Christmas carol sing-along after dinner.

2. Drive together or walk together through a neighborhood that has beautiful lights and enjoy the display.

3. Go see an outdoor nativity display in your area.

4. Make a treat together—perhaps warm cocoa with marshmallows or cookies.

5. Read a Christmas storybook together. In our home, we read one every night starting December 1 as one of our family traditions.

6. Make stockings out of colored paper and have family members write compliments to slip in each other's stockings all day long.

7. Sing several Primary songs about Jesus together.

8. Watch a Christmas video—*The Nativity* is an excellent one.

9. Visit with grandparents—in person or over the Internet—and share Christmas memories.

10. Make ornaments together or other decorations for the tree. Easy ideas can be found on the Internet. An easy one is to have each family member color a picture of the birth of Jesus on a 3" x 5" card and hang from a ribbon. You can get small inexpensive frames and mount the picture on cardstock, cut to fit, if you'd like.

11. Have everyone get in their jammies. Put on fun music (we love *Mitch Miller Christmas* or the Beatles) and have a family dance in the family room. Go crazy and have fun with this one!

12. Wrap up warm and go to a beautiful place to watch the sunset together and talk about what Christmas means to you.

Conclusion

Most families have specific Christmas traditions that they celebrate every year. Perhaps this year, in addition to your favorites, you might like to start a new tradition. Here are a few ideas to consider. Each of these ideas will help you to memorialize your experience giving gifts to the Savior. Feel free to pick and choose what works for you.

PRESENTS

My niece Kacy shared with me their family tradition. She purchases a garland that is made up of tiny gift boxes in shiny colors. She trims the boxes off the garland and puts them into a large clear bowl. Next to the bowl, she places a beautiful box.

During the entire month of December, as family members perform one of their "gifts" to Jesus, they take a little present box from the bowl and transfer it to the beautiful box. On Christmas, the family opens the box and celebrates all the gifts they have given to the Savior all month long.

BOX DISPLAY

Place a giant, beautifully wrapped box on a table or under the Christmas tree, and next to it, prominently display a picture of Christ. As family members perform a "gift," invite them to fill out slips of paper describing their "gift," sign their name, and put it into the box.

Another idea is to have beautiful boxes under the tree for each member of the family. On each box is a tag with that family member's favorite picture of Christ (a variety of pictures are available at the LDS Church Distribution center). Family members jot down their "gifts" on slips of paper and put them into their box throughout the experience.

Christmas Journal

Invite family members to keep a Christmas journal. They could designate a page (or more) for each of the gifts they would like to give to the Savior, and throughout the days, months, or year, they can write down what they have done to give those gifts to the Savior. They can also write about their own experiences and growth in the process.

Gift Calendar

Post a special calendar in a prominent location where your whole family can see it. Invite family members to jot down a note on each calendar day when they give a gift to Christ.

Straw

A common way to memorialize the gifts we give to Jesus is to set up an empty manger with a container of straw nearby. As each person performs a kind act, they put a piece of straw into the manger, with the baby Jesus being placed there on Christmas Eve.

Giving Tree

Set up a small Christmas tree on a tabletop or mantel. Decorate it with small boxes tied with ribbon. Inside each box is a slip of paper with a service or a random act of kindness to perform, such as, "Give out five smiles to strangers today," or "Tell three people what you like about them." Each day select one box and perform the gift of kindness written inside.

Paper Chain

Start a paper chain out of colored paper strips. Place extra paper strips in a box next to the chain. As family members share their "gift," invite them to write it down on a paper strip and loop it into the chain. This is a wonderful tradition the family can work on all year long. Imagine the giant garland of love that you've worked on all year long looping your Christmas tree!

PICTURE OF CHRIST

This idea is a favorite of young children. Display a framed picture of Christ in their room. Get a package of tiny happy-face stickers. As the child performs a "gift" for Jesus, he or she can put a sticker on the frame each night before they go to bed. Soon Jesus will be surrounded by smiley faces!

•   •   •

Each of these ideas can help you focus on giving gifts to the Savior. The important part of the process is to focus on Him and to help you remember Him.

I hope you enjoy the experiences you have this Christmas season as you explore ways you can give gifts to Christ. I hope this will help you come unto Him and feel of His love.

About the Author

MERRILEE BOYACK is a popular speaker at BYU Education Week and at Time Out for Women conferences. She is an estate-planning attorney who conducts her part-time law practice from her home. Merrilee and her husband are the parents of four sons.